Why Terrorism
Continues in the Philippines?

Why Terrorism Continues in the Philippines?

The Causes of Continous Terrorism in the Philippines?

Mr. Ano Who

To order additional copies of this book, contact:
Xlibris
1-888-795-4274
www.Xlibris.com
Orders@Xlibris.com
663528

CONTENTS

TO MY WIFE, to my children, especially to my dear granddaughter, Shiley, and to my future grandchildren. I may never have a chance to meet and see them anymore, for my life may be shortened soon, but I want to let them know that I love them too. It has been my dream to build a haven surrounded by my little ones and awakened by their loving hugs.

ACKNOWLEDGMENT

M Y DEAREST APPRECIATION to my professors at the American Military University who contributed so much knowledge about disaster management, terrorism, national security, and intelligence studies and analysis during my school years. The knowledge I have learned while this book is in progress will remain in my heart and mind forever.

To my alma mater, American Military University, an American public university system in Charles Town, West Virginia, USA, including all the people who had shared so much information and the ability to do research that led to the writing of this book, and to all my friends and people who had contributed molding my life, that made me of who I am today. To them, I offer my salute and deepest gratitude, and above all, to our Almighty God who had created all things beneath and above the earth for the protection, life, and provision he never fails to give, my thanks and appreciation, worship and honor, all belongs to Him!

PREFACE

I HAVE TRAVELED BY land, air, and sea from the northernmost part of the Philippines down to Tawi-Tawi Islands. My journey included the most dangerous sail I have embarked on—dressed as a Muslim and my name changed to a Muslim name—to Semporna and Tawau in Sabah, Malaysia. My experiences on this journey are expressed in this book. During this journey, I heard different sounds of languages or dialects, and I saw the regionalized culture of Filipinos, how living in different islands contributed to the disunity and cultural barriers within their race. This exposure to the different living conditions of the people of the islands of Luzon, Visayas, and Mindanao, particularly in Jolo and Tawi-Tawi, Sulu, corroborates with serious issues as possible root cause of hundreds of years of grievances, rebellion, and terrorism in the country. I heard personal accounts of grievances against race, religions, politics, and governments from Muslims and Christians.

On my way to Sabah, Malaysia, I lived with the Tausug Muslim people in different small islands of Sulu without power and fresh water except rain. We did island hopping for about a week and stayed in small islands before crossing the sea line bordering the Philippines and Malaysia.

Under the light of the full moon, I was settling on the crystal white sand, looking beyond the calm waters, watching the clear and beautiful starry skies amazed by the splendor of God's creation. In the midst of it all, I began to wonder why God's special ones, created in his image, are neglected and living in less than desirable conditions. Truly, the inhabitants in the islands Sulu are not living; they are just trying to survive. Seeing this, I could say that we are living in a world so unfair. Their state of living made them susceptible to ideologies empowered with weapons and hopeless promises. The inhabitants in the region are living in an island with pristine white sand in the middle of almost endless, vast, and wide-ocean but don't realize the value of what they have. They seemed contented living far in making their dreams a reality. Foreigners and tourists could have treasured the gorgeousness of the islands, but it's sad to note when I heard them saying, "You can take our wives away but not our guns." It's a thought of survival for life on a desperate situation for people not realizing that beyond that stormy sea, there's always hope for a new day, a rising sun with golden rays, an emblem of hope and prosperity. For about a month, I ate and stayed with them in the islands without power and fresh water except rain.

We rode in a small wooden boat called *tempel* by the Tausug Muslims as a means of transportation going to Semporna, Sabah, Malaysia, from Sitangkai, Tawi-Tawi, Sulu. There were about twenty people in the *tempel* going to Sabah, Malaysia, and I was the only Christian in the group. The Muslim boat operator changed my Christian name to a Muslim name to avoid suspicion upon arrival in Sabah, Malaysia.

While sailing through high tide and low tide, I saw the amazing underwater mountains – a mid-ocean ridge that remarkably reveals the colorful and lovely creatures under the sea. My heart exclaimed, "What a treasure for Philippine tourism development!" when I saw the beauty of nature in the small islands with bright white sand surrounded by the bluish ocean.

Without the peace and order situation in the Southern Philippines, these islands could have been a tourist attraction and could have boosted the economy in the region. The Muslim citizens should realize the value and the importance of peace and order in their community to alleviate their economic condition.

From Sitangkai Island, it only takes two to four hours in a small machine boat going to Semporna, but since we did island hopping, it took us longer to reach the last small island closed to the border line of Sabah and Sulu, Philippines. In a small island we embarked and stayed, we lay down and rested on an open ground with few palm trees. I was led to dig deep and search for the causes of terrorism in the Philippines, and I wrote this book for the readers to uncover why the struggle of the Muslims in Southern Philippines lingers. The chosen title for this book comes from my heart and mind as I continue to explore for answers why terrorism in this country never ends. I may fail to mention all the reasons for rebellion or terrorism in the country, but to name a few at least maybe enough to show why terrorism continues in the Philippines. In my extensive research and years of traveling throughout the country, I found reasons why the killings and kidnappings are rampant and terrorism remains. It is my hope that you, readers, may find this book challenging and revealing.

INTRODUCTION

O N SEPTEMBER 11, 2001, terrible news surprised and scared the whole world. America, the superpower, and the most influential country in the entire world, was under attack. The terrorists hijacked two of American planes, American Airlines Flight 11 and the United Airlines Flight 175, and crashed them into the North and South Towers of the World Trade Center. The towers collapsed and killed about three thousand people. It was confirmed that the culprit for this terrible incident are terrorists. The intelligence community never ever anticipated that the terrorists could use an American airplane as a weapon against the United States. This event marked the war against terrorism, and many nations responded; the Philippines was the first in line. It made America stretch its muscle against terrorism abroad.

The Philippines is a nation known to be rich in natural resources, culture, and tradition, but it is also known to be a haven of bandits, terrorists, and communists. A group of bandits, believed to be terrorists linked to Al-Qaeda, a group formed by Osama Bin Laden, the most known terrorist of all time, nested in the small island of Sulu in Mindanao, endangering the lives of the people in and around the island and is threatening national security. The United States of America, leading the war against terror, did not leave the Philippines' terrorism problem unattended. They sent out millions of US military aid to advance the equipment and training of the Philippine military. Instead of fastening the elimination of terrorism, it continuously and aggressively prevails, and the Philippine military remains unsophisticated, while the terrorist group is getting high-powered weapons suspiciously acquired from the Philippine military. Then a question arose: Did the foreign financial aid help the elimination of terrorism, or it did fuel the war, like fanning a dying fire? This book reveals the causes of the continuous terrorism in the Philippines, and it scrutinizes the three colonial periods—Spanish, American, and Japanese occupations—on how these contributed to the rise of rebellion and terrorism in the country. This book precisely defines the meaning of "rebellion" and "terrorism," speculates the role of the Philippine colonizers in the formation of the Filipinos' anti-colonialism spirit, reveals the reason behind the formation of resistant groups, and exposes the reason for the continuous terrorism in the country despite foreign aids. Not to mention the South China Sea disputes against, America and other countries should evaluate whether it is right to focus on the needs of the Philippine military or it should rather give attention to advancing Philippine education and economic development.

CHAPTER 1

Terrorism and Rebellion Denotation

TERRORISM AND REBELLION have a slight difference in meaning. Therefore, understanding these two words is important before we can differentiate and use them correctly. This very thin difference could easily be ignored or misunderstood by attributing rebellion to terrorism. According to *Merriam-Webster, rebellion* is

- *An effort by many people to change the government or leader of a country by the use of protest or violence.*
- *Open opposition toward a person or group in authority.*
- *Refusal to obey rules or accept normal standards of behavior, dress, etc.*[1]

To some Filipinos, the word *insurgency* most likely understood as synonymous to *rebellion* especially during the Spanish regime:

> *"Insurgency is rebellion; revolt; the state of being insurgents, while insurrection is an organized opposition to an authority; a mutiny; a rebellion."*[2]

It refers to the discontented citizens against the Philippine government. As a result, terror existed when rebel groups arose in some areas in the archipelago and when they became internationally linked with Al-Qaeda.

The term *rebellion* may imply to domestic issues with political implications resulting to rebellious acts.

Terrorism, on the other hand, according to the US Department of Defense Dictionary of Military and Associated Terms, means

> *"The unlawful use of violence or threat of violence to instill fear and coerce governments or societies. Terrorism is often motivated by religious, political, or other ideological beliefs and committed in the pursuit of goals that are usually political."*[3]

Another article, "The Alternative to Wars. Terrorism and Politics: Definition to Terrorism," defines *terrorism* as,

> *"Destruction of people or property not acting on behalf of an established government for the purpose of redressing a real or imaginary injustice attributed to an established government and aimed directly or indirectly at an established government."*[4]

The term terrorism is widely used internationally, with implications to Al-Qaeda or any Al-Qaeda-linked groups, not acting for an established government nor representing a country.

Who are the terrorists?

In the above definition of *terrorism*, the personalities that can be considered terrorists also have their meaning of such word. They never call themselves terrorists. An Islamic extremist view was used to broaden their meaning of the word *terrorism*. Osama Bin Laden, an internationally known terrorist leader who opposed American and Western ideology, expressed his side about being called terrorists during an interview with Peter Arnett, a CNN reporter who went into the mountains above Jalalabad in March 1997. Peter Arnett went into a blanket-lined mud hut to meet and interview Bin Laden. In his interview with Arnett, Bin Laden used the word *terrorist* to describe the president of the United States. He complained and accused the United States of setting up a double standard. He said that the United States want to invade other countries to steal natural resources and to impose guns that would rule such nation and want that same nation's approval, and they are called terrorists in case that government hesitates and disagrees with it.[5] Osama Bin Laden, in his statement, opposed the existing belief about which the real terrorists are and accused Pres. George W. Bush as the worst terrorist. On top of it, an article labeled both US President George W. Bush and British Prime Minister Tony Blair as the world's leading terrorists,[6] citing the definition of the Federal Bureau of Investigation (FBI). According to the FBI, terrorism is;

> *"An unlawful force of violence against persons or property to intimidate or coerce a government, the civilian population, or any segment thereof in furtherance of political or social objectives.[7]"*

Based on FBI's definition, M. Schiller declared both the US President George W. Bush and British Prime Minister Tony Blair as terrorists since their acts equaled to such definition. His write-ups also described the most damaging effects of war with the US mighty weapons, which caused many casualties and had created fear and terror, inflicting the hearts and minds of the civilians involved. He considered it "worse than terrorism," with millions, if not billions, of dollars' worth of losses in infrastructures.[8]

During Pres. George W. Bush's visit to Indonesia, the world's most Muslim-populated nation, he was confronted with a massive protest and was called a war criminal and a terrorist.[9] If both parties called each other terrorist, then what is the real definition of terrorism and who are to be considered terrorists? The word *intent* or *motive* divides the two parties into separate ends. It's the intention of individuals or group of insurgents that identifies who could be considered terrorists. The United States is a nation bound to promote democracy, human rights, and freedom from a tyrant and oppressive leader. When sanctioned by the United States Congress or United Nations, she is ready to respond to countries who seek assistance. The United States may create fear and terror in response to a country's demand for help and protection, while the Al-Qaeda-linked group is not an established country, nor acting on behalf of a country. Their goal is to coerce and create fear or terror to impose their ideology. The United States did not intend to use its power to create fear and to terrorize any nations. Instead, their real purpose is to liberate countries threatened or invaded by their neighbors and of course protect America's interest and security. However, Al-Qaeda-linked groups created a movement driven by their extreme fanaticism and extremism. Their intent is to instigate and impose the forming and linking of domestic groups to carry out their ideology and extreme beliefs and to terrorize people. Through terror, they exist.

The United States did not terrorize, claim, invade, or occupy a nation, and neither do they intend to possess a nation's land, oil, or other natural resources. The United States' responses to the terrorist attack on September 11, 2001, and its involvement in foreign nations' wars against their invaders or oppressors, as a response to their call for help, are just acts of a big brother. The United States liberated Kuwait from Saddam Hussein's invasion and returned it to its legitimate leaders. The all-out war on terror was just a response to the 9/11 incident. The same thing happened to the Philippines when the United States granted it its independence and restored the leadership to the Filipinos and left them to rule. The US invasion of Iraq had been approved by International Congress, and right now, Iraq is back in the hands of their national leaders. After the conquest of Kuwait and Saddam Hussein took control, he made it an annex or a province of Iraq. Kuwait asked the United States for military assistance, and again, America returned it to its legitimate government. Without America's assistance and involvement, Kuwait would have been history.[10] The United States would never steal the oil and resources of other countries. In fact, America has her own oil deposit more than enough oil deposit compared to other allied democratic industrialized nations are much bigger markets of petroleum than the Middle East. Although America was involved in Afghanistan's war against the Taliban and Al-Qaeda that control their lands, America did not take advantage of it and was never interested in getting their oil. In fact, the United States has more oil deposit and sources of alternative energy. America just wanted to promote democracy and punish the terrorists responsible for the 9/11 incident and the conflicting countries believed to be harboring and have been supporting terrorism. The above accusation is a black propaganda against the United States. Jahanzeb Hussein, author of an article, explained that America's invasion of Afghanistan in 2001 was not about getting their gas, oil, or other resources but to "flex its power muscles" in punishing countries responsible for the 9/11 incident.

Those nations, who are in alliance with the terrorists or who harbored terrorism shall take the penalty.[11]

In response to the 9/11 incident, Pres. George W. Bush sounded off from the White House and repeatedly emphasized in his televised speeches that the United States is against any countries harboring terrorism or being allies with terrorists. The United States is interested only on targeting nations that are havens for terrorists. As a leader and defender of human rights, justice, and freedom in the world, the United States felt obligated in protecting nations that ask help in liberating their oppressed men and women from their tyrant leaders. Instead of receiving an honor for a heroic act, America was criticized and misunderstood. Examining the case of the Holocaust, the killings of hundreds of thousands of Jews by Adolf Hitler, it would not have happened had the United States immediately responded to their cry for help. Because of America's failure to bomb the Germans' concentration camps, the Holocaust happened, and the United States was blamed for their failure to come to rescue. A Washington DC journalist, K. C. Gleason, commented on the United States' failure to act on the rescue of the Jewish people from the hands of Hitler in Germany. Gleason said that United States shared the blame for the Holocaust, that there are American officials well aware of Hitler's crime during the World War II yet they chose to be apathetic about it.[12] At this point, America had been blamed for their noninvolvement in the war against Germany that could have prevented the Jewish genocide. Susan D. Glazer, a journalist, wrote an article about the German Italian insurgence during World War Two. She was also quoted that for more than twenty years, Auschwitz, the most infamous of the death camps, has become a symbol of the Holocaust. The name Auschwitz has come to represent not only the horrors of the Nazi genocidal regime but also the failure of the US government to take appropriate action to prevent the murder of millions of people.[13]

However, in recent years, America had been taking the call to fight for countries that need help. The United States had already lost hundreds of thousand young lives in battle, liberating many oppressed nations that sought help from them. Many wounded men and women sacrificed their lives when called to protect America and the citizens of the world against tyranny and dictatorship.

Notwithstanding with America's economic depression and its citizens who suffered as a result of a war, the American people still took the responsibility, as the bearer of justice and freedom in the world protecting nation's and citizen's human rights and liberating women from the hands of their oppressive or dictatorship governments. After liberating them, as in Iraq, America's sacrifice continued and supported them regarding financial assistance, reconstruction, infrastructure development, restoration, education and continued security and military aid even at the height of US economic crisis. As confirmed by CBSNews.com Website, an individual auditor submitted a final report to the US Congress that about $60 billion were allegedly wasted while rebuilding Iraq. The article further narrated,

> *"To date, the U.S. has spent more than $60 billion in reconstruction grants to help Iraq get back on its feet after the country was broken by "more than two decades of war, sanctions and dictatorship. That works out to about $15 million a day. And yet Iraq's government is rife with corruption and infighting. The near-daily deadly bombings cowed the Bagdad's streets. A quarter of the country's 31 million population lives in poverty and few have reliable electricity and clean water. Overall, including all military and diplomatic costs and other aid, the U.S. has spent at least $767 billion since the American-led invasion, according to the Congressional Budget Office. National Priorities Project, a U.S. research group that analyzes federal data, estimated the cost at $811 billion, noting that some funds are still being spent on ongoing projects."*[14]

It's never been heard that the terrorists spent much money to help the economically poor nations for literacy, education, and economic development, but they caused killings, destructions, terror, and fear. Neither they were heard sending assistance and help during disasters and calamities. They are known when there are killings and bombings, but they are never heard of sending help to save lives. Thus, Osama Bin Laden's accusations against the United States and Al-Qaeda's terroristic movements are unjustifiable. The United States is just trying to do its duty to fight an oppressive government, set the people free, and continue rebuilding them even when the war is over. Therefore, this discussion proves who the true terrorists are—those described by their intentions revealed in their actions.

CHAPTER 2

A Glimpse of Philippine History

A. **The First Spanish Settlement in the Philippines**

THE PHILIPPINE HISTORIAN, Teodoro A. Agocillio, stated in his book that Spain "rediscovered" the Philippines in 1521. It was during the opening of European shipping driven not only by propellers but also the cravings of two competing superpowers: Portugal and Spain. Voyagers were sent out to explore the globe, trying to widen their territory for "gold and glory" in the guise of spreading the "gospel or Roman Catholicism."[15] The Spanish rule over the country brought the Filipinos to experience severe economic, political, and social suppression. The Spaniards only brought a few limited useful contributions in terms of educational and governmental systems. For almost three hundred years, the Spaniards brought suffering, pain, and fear to the Filipinos. There were racial discrimination, suppression of human rights, abuse of power, exploitation, and corruption during those times.

1. *The Spaniards' Divide-and-Rule System*

The Spaniards did not train Filipino leaders. Instead, they imposed oppressive divide-and-rule system of governance for about three hundred years. The geography of the 7,107 islands comprising the archipelago and the varying cultures of the Filipinos in different regions may have contributed to the disunity among them and made it easier for the Spaniards to divide and control the people. Nonetheless, for potential Filipino leaders, education became a dream that led them to study abroad. In the absence of a strong centralized government in the country, the Spaniards took advantage of the regionalized Filipino cultures and disunity. However, each island had its traditional system of government and leaders. Then again, under the brutal and abusive colonizer, it was just very difficult for Filipinos to unite their forces against their intruders. Because of lack of unity and national leadership, the Spaniards effectively imposed the divide-and-rule governance while no one could lead an amalgamated force to rise against the Spanish regime.[16]

2. *The Spanish Oppression and Injustices*

The middle-class Filipinos aimed for more economic and political power but were prevented from achieving more in life no matter how qualified the Filipinos were. The Spaniards made them ignorant, fanatic, and powerless to rise against them. Many middle-class families had been victims of the injustices of Spanish friars who made their living miserable. Later, the Filipino grievances escalated that led the concerned Filipinos to form a group called Illustrates as the spokesman of the oppressed masses who desired for reform.

The priesthood was considered the most prestigious career among Filipino families. They dreamed to have family members enter the ministry, but the Spaniards refused to, discouraged, and refrained from ordaining Filipinos into priesthood.

The Cavite Mutiny in 1872 was a staged mutiny led by Sergeant La Madrid with a group of Filipino soldiers and laborers against Governor Izquierdo at the Spanish arsenal, but the small group was quickly subdued by the Spanish authority. Many Filipinos agitating reforms were persecuted, arrested, jailed, and executed on the suspicion that they were part of the mutiny. Father Gomez, Father Burgos, and Father Zamora (GOMBURZA)—the three priests implicated in the revolt—were convicted and sentenced to death by *garrote*, which means to die by stick beatings, at the Luneta Park on February 17, 1872. The archbishop of Manila, Militon Martinez, declared that the three Filipino priests were innocent. Filipino priests were discriminated. The death of the three priests escalated their grievances. Driven by economic greed and desire for more wealth and power, the Spanish friars and rulers became abusive, and they committed injustices to the natives.[17]

The GOMBURZA priests died as martyrs by making a stand on what they believed what was right before God and men. They deserved to be called heroes of faith and should be canonized as saints according to the dogma of the Roman Catholic Church,[18] but surely, the Roman church could not afford to produce saints out of these three great men of faith, who had suffered tortures and garrote beatings and died in the hands of Spanish Roman Catholic friars.

3. *Religious Bigotry, Ritualism, and Fanaticism – Effective Tools for Heart and Mind Control*

The Spaniards, under Ferdinand Magellan's command, arrived in the Philippines armed with Roman Catholicism and high-powered cannons. The propagation of Catholicism introduced religious ritualism or fanaticism that were similar to the pagan worship or rituals that old folks do even up to these days. Before the Spaniards brought the Roman Catholic religion in the Philippines, the pagan natives worshipped graven images, stones, trees, etc., wherefore, and the natives readily adopted Roman Catholicism for some similarities to pagan worship. Evidently, religion became an effective weapon that controlled the hearts and minds of fanatic and superstitious Filipinos. It is a form of mind control. Teodoro A. Agoncillo, a Filipino historian, explained that during pre-Spanish time, the Filipino tribes had rituals and practices of their own. They worship "anitos" or the believed spirits of their dead ancestors, relatives, and friends. These are tantamount to the adoration of the dead saints in the Roman Catholic Church. Agoncillo further said that the ancient Filipinos believed in the immortality of the soul and life after death. They also believed in "Bathalang Maykapal" and a host of ranking deities, such as the god of farming, god of war, god of fire, goddess of the harvest, god of hell, god of love, god of the rainbow, and gods of other functions in life. The "Bathala" is the superior god, or "Dios" in Spanish, who was the creator of man, heavens, and earth. The veneration of soul-spirits was a common practice called "cult of the dead." They carved idols of stones, gold, and images of their dead relatives and offered their favorite foods or wines when they were still alive for they would be offended if not shared with them and afraid they would take vengeance on the living by inflicting them with illnesses or diseases.[19] Instead of converting the people to a true Christian belief, the

Spanish priests did not eradicate these native pagan rituals. Instead, they adapted them into the Roman Catholic Church practices, and there are continued until today. Agoncillo said,

> *"These beliefs, religious and otherwise, were not eradicated with the coming of Western civilization. Most of them practiced behind the backs of Christian missionaries, with the result that side by side with Catholicism, elements of paganism survived and penetrated the new religion. Today, in many rural areas and even in some big cities, the practice of Catholicism is a curious mixture of Christian and pagan beliefs, thereby making Filipino Catholicism unique."*[20]

The compromising strategy of the Roman Catholic religion or the Spaniards is evident that they are more after the widening of their territories rather than teaching the true gospel. The similarities of the religious system to the native pagan rituals made it easy to win the religious allegiance of the natives in the islands. They adopted a similar form of worship that made the people comfortable. Because the Filipinos are superstitious, it was easy for the Spaniards to effectively imposing religious rituals and practices; it made the natives feel secured, scared of the consequences that might fall on them if they do otherwise. At that point, religion was a good weapon to win the minds and hearts of the people. Up to these days, many Filipinos are fanatics and demonstrate annual religious ritualism. "Sinulog" is an example of pre-Spanish form of ritual that originated from the natives of Cebu, which they have inherited from their ancestors. The Roman Catholic Church turned it into a church practice and tradition that attracted many religious people. Filipino Roman Catholics coming from different islands travel to Cebu for the annual Sinulog celebration not realizing that they embraced paganism. Many of pagan system of worship and practices were adapted and integrated into the Roman Catholic Church and religiously practiced by devotees. With spirit of fanaticism and the fear of non-compliance of the required rituals, their mind, body, and soul became totally submissive unto the religious system of worship. They even bowed down and tend to worship the Spanish friars. The spirit of pagan "emperor worship" of Rome emerged to the first Christian Church in Rome and passed it down to the priests or bishops, then "Popes," as supreme pontiff. They have learned to bow and kiss the hand of priests when they meet them on the street, and it is still being practiced by some Filipinos even to these days. Upon the arrival of the pope at the Manila International Airport, now Ninoy Aquino International Airport, the deposed strong man, the late Pres. Ferdinand E. Marcos, bowed on the ground before the pope and kissed his feet and hands.

In one instance also, I had seen my uncle who was a lawyer and once a congressman and mayor of a city publicly bow down before the monsignor when we met him in a restaurant. He openly bowed down before the priest and kissed his hands and feet. The priest condoned the gesture of worship in contrary to Apostle Peter and all followers of the Lord God who refused these acts. The apostles refused people to bow before them. When Cornelius bowed before him, Peter responded, saying, "Stand up, I myself also a man."[21]

During their missionary journey to Lystra, St. Paul and Barnabas were worshiped by the people, but they refused to be worshiped, tore their clothes, and cried out, "Men, why are you doing these things? We also are men with the same nature as you, and preach to you that you should turn from these vain things to the living God . . ."[22]

In another instance, even the holy angels refused to be worshipped when St. John bowed before the angel, but the angel said, "See that you do not do that! I am your fellow servant and of your brethren who have the testimony of Jesus. Worship God!"[23]

The response is "Worship God!" It belongs to God alone. These practice infiltrated the early Christian church in Rome, now the Roman Catholic Church, resulting from a mixture of paganism and Christianity. When the Emperor Constantine the Great made the Roman Catholic Church the one official and dominant religion in the entire Roman Empire, they tried to embrace all religion just to accommodate all into the Christian Church which turned Roman Catholic Church. It paved the way for Roman pagan cultic traditions slowly crept into the Christian church in Rome, including pagan "emperor worship" conveyed to the pope. A document explained that,

> "As the Romans extended their dominance throughout the Mediterranean world, their policy in general was to absorb the deities and cults of other peoples rather than try to eradicate them, since they believed that preserving tradition promoted

social stability . . . Public vows formerly made for the security of
the republic now were directed at the wellbeing of the emperor.
So-called "emperor worship" expanded on a grand scale the
traditional Roman veneration of the ancestral dead and of the
Genius, the divine tutelary of every individual. Imperial cult
became one of the major ways Rome advertised its presence
in the provinces and cultivated shared cultural identity and
loyalty throughout the Empire. Rejection of the state religion
was tantamount to treason . . ."[24]

The public bowing to the pope or priests was derived from emperor worship practice and passed on to the Filipinos. It led them to submission and respect to the Spanish friars. Their minds and hearts are now controlled to obey whatever the Roman church tells them to do. The native Filipinos may not be afraid of their swords and canons, but they are scared of not paying the highest respect to a crucifix and graven images rather than the meaning or the person behind it, even to the priests. The Spaniards used the cross on the left and a sword on the right if Filipinos refused to submit.

Spain and Portugal were two rival powers in reaching the eastern part of the world to win new lands in a guise of religious mission; they are motivated by the three Gs—gospel, gold, and glory.[25] With their superior strategy to interact with the inhabitants, their high-powered weapons, and their Roman Catholic religion, they won the faith and allegiance of the early Filipinos. The Spaniards offered friendship and used religion as a façade and the high-powered canon as an alternative when somebody refused to submit.

General McArthur wanted to use similar strategy after Japan surrendered. He realized that religion was a proven and effective way to win people. MacArthur attempted to use religion to change the Japanese mind. After defeating Japan in WWII, he wanted to send thousands of Christian missionaries and Bibles to Japan to fill its emptiness, believing that Christianity could open more opportunities for reform in their fanatic mind, and even considered converting Emperor Hirohito to Christianity.[26]

The same tactics were used by Osama Bin Laden when he used Islamic fanaticism or extremism to brainwash the minds of his followers and trainees. These caused them to submit religiously to his ideology even to the extent of sacrificing their lives as suicide bombers. Michael Eber, a counterterrorism specialist, wrote,

> *"Osama Bin Laden has taken over the minds of thousands of Muslim Fundamentalists. He holds the power to call for terrorist attacks at any time. How did he achieve this power and how has he maintained it with such a large amount of people? He has gotten so many people to follow his teachings, which he is the world's most sought after terrorist. Bin Laden uses religious fanaticism, as a front for his mission."[27]*

Once the people's conviction is rooted down into their hearts and mind, they could give up their lives to stand for what they believe. Suicide bombers were victims of these religious brainwashing techniques. The Islamic teaching taught that if Muslims can kill a nonbeliever and died doing it for Allah, they will have seven-two virgins to engage with a special treatment in paradise.[28]

In this extreme and lustful type of teachings of extremist Osama Bin Laden, the narrow-minded lazy individuals who don't want to work hard to support their families could easily commit and submit themselves without analyzing the consequences. The financial promises from terrorist leader Bin Laden or his successors became enticing bait to lazy jobless people. It made them more than willing to leave their ugly wives and problematic families to go and kill Westerners or non-Muslims with a dream to live in paradise surrounded by many beautiful virgins. No wonder why suicide bombers are coming out with a bomb wrapped around their bodies and explode in crowded areas. It sounds crazy, but truly it's a form of heart and mind control to let narrow-minded and less educated people willingly lay down their lives. Religious fanaticism and bigotry are useful and effective tools for heart and mind control.

B. Spanish-American War in the Philippines

When the Spanish-American War broke out, the Filipinos took it as an opportunity to liberate themselves from Spanish tyranny. The Filipinos helped the Americans by providing them intelligence information against the Spaniards. With the developing good Filipino-American relationship, the Americans summoned the exiled president of the First Philippine Republic, Emilio Aguinaldo, to return to Manila from Hong Kong. Eventually, Emilio Aguinaldo supported the Americans by leading Filipino military forces against Spaniards in Luzon. Emilio Aguinaldo returned to the Philippines with anticipation of Philippine independence from the rule of the Spaniards with the help of Americans. Aguinaldo formed the Filipino forces to fight side by side with the Americans, but it was sad to note that when the Spaniards lost the war with the Filipinos as front fighters, Adm. George Dewey conspired with the Spaniards and convinced them to surrender to America, not to the first Philippine republic. The Filipinos felt betrayed, and the long-sought independence remained to be a dream for every Filipino. The Filipino military diverted the bloody fight against the American army when the first shot incident happened. It ignited the three-year bloody Filipino-American War, from 1899 to 1902.[29]

C. **Filipino-American War Ignited**

The Filipino-American War was the first Filipino colonial war with a world power. After it defeated Spain in the Philippines and Cuba in 1898, the United States purchased Puerto Rico, Philippines, and several islands from the Spain. Since the Filipinos had been fighting a bloody revolution against Spain since 1896, they did not expect of another imperialist colonial power.[30]

1. *The First Shot at San Juan Bridge*

When the American troops landed in the Philippines in 1889, it was a ploy to help the local rebels overthrow their Spanish colonial oppressors. However, when the Americans achieved victory, they took control of the nation. They turned their guns toward their Filipino friends, denying them even a say for their own nation's future; they attacked the Filipino people. The war between the occupying American army and the Filipino forces broke out when a Filipino soldier at the bridge was shot by American soldier, Pvt. William Grayson. Later along the way, the story changed for whatever reason, and the mark of the first shoot at the bridge was transferred to the corner of Sociego corner Silencio Streets, Santa Mesa District, Manila.[31]

The motive of changing the mark and location may be doubtful, and it created an impression to cover the real cause of the Filipino-American War. It could have been more historically significant if the truth of the shooting incident remained at the bridge. The bridge may become a historical landmark as to what ignited the Fil-Am War; it would symbolize the Filipino courage to fight for sovereignty.

According to the first story, the three-year Filipino-American War was ignited by a shot at the bridge, when Pvt. William Grayson shot a Filipino soldier trying to cross. It happened when the American soldiers restricted the Filipino soldiers from entering the Manila Spanish Garrison after its capture. Accordingly, the Filipino soldiers got offended when they were prohibited from entering the area after they fought side by side with them. The issue of sovereignty possibly peaked at that time. The fatal shooting was followed by an immediate US military offensive aggression against Filipinos, and it marked the beginning of the Filipino-American War, which lasted from 1899 to 1902 until Gen. William Howard Taft established a civilian colonial government. This gruesome cruelty, heartlessness, vicious, and mercilessness of American genocide killed thousands of innocent Filipinos, including kids, and this was not sufficiently recorded or written in Philippine history. Filipinos were once described as less human by Americans. At the height of his madness, Gen. Jacob H. Smith reduced the category of the Filipino people to the level of animals and ordered his men to slaughter the Filipinos:

> *"A little bit better than a dog, a noisome reptiles in some instance, whose best disposition was a rubbish heap . . . I want no prisoners. I wish you to kill and burn. The more you kill and burn the better. It will please me".*[32]

The Filipinos suspected that the shooting incident at the bridge was premeditated because it occurred two days before the US Congress ratified the Treaty of Paris on February 6, 1899, which proclaimed that Spain officially ceded the Philippines, Guam, and Puerto Rico to the United States for the amount of $20 million only. The shooting incident, as suspected, may have supported the move of the pro-annexationists to ratify the treaty for the United States' acquisition of the Philippines against the anti-imperialists. This three-year Filipino-American War did not leave enough published documents with complete and detailed information about the life of Filipinos at this time. Despite of this tyranny, the Filipino guerillas helplessly fought back, but in 1900, the Americans declared martial law to combat guerrilla warfare.

In Samar, Leyte, a massacre was committed in the small village of Balalinga. As ordered by Gen. Jacob H. Smith, the American soldiers killed, tortured, and shot down anybody capable of carrying weapons, including boys above ten years old. Samar turned into a"howling wilderness" at that time. During those days, hatred against American prejudice had grievously developed and deposited in the hearts and minds of the Filipinos. Hundreds of thousands of lives were lost in just three years of conflicts.[33]

2. *American Campaign of Brutality*

During the American brutality campaign against the Filipinos, they expected the Fil-Am War would shorten because of their superior and powerful weapons but surprised when it lasted to three years. They got shocked by the courage and persistence of the Filipino guerrilla warriors. Although with limited firearms, the guerrilla's familiarity with the country's terrain gave them the advantage that dragged the Fil-Am War to several years, sustained by the unyielding determination to defend the country. In some locations, American flag was displayed and waved as the symbol of victory, but the guerrillas continued fighting and were secretly supported by the residents. The people posted as category peasant class residents during the day but revolutionaries by night. It was very dangerous for Americans to be seen outside their garrison or else be killed by the guerrillas and their supporters. To combat Filipino guerrilla warfare, the Americans declared martial law at the end of 1900 but started a "scorch-earth pacification campaign."

They called the Filipinos nigger and considered every Filipino—male, female, or child—an enemy who could already carry weapons. They made the entire community or town responsible for the guerrillas' actions, and mere objection to the Americans were considered treason. People were tortured and killed, and villages suspected sympathetic to guerrillas were burned. They introduced a "reconcentration policy" by putting the entire population into concentration camps to isolate the people from the guerrillas and to cut material assistance to guerrillas.

The camp, without good sanitation, was packed with people; it became a good breeding ground for "cholera," a deadly disease that caused illness and death to many people. Those found outside the camp were considered guerrillas. In Batangas alone, more than one hundred thousand died from fighting and from being imprisoned in the concentration camp.[34]

D. **The Japanese Vicious Regime**

The Filipinos believe that the Philippines became the battle ground of the American – Japanese war in WWII. On December 8, 1941, Japan bombed the Pearl Harbor. Hours after the Pearl Harbor bombing, Japan invaded the Philippines, and between 1942 and 1945, the Japanese Empire occupied the Philippine Commonwealth Government. The US aircraft at Pearl Harbor was severely damaged by the surprise attack and bombardments of the Japanese. The American Asiatic fleet stationed in the Philippines departed to Java for safety, and on the night of March 11, 1942, Gen. Douglas MacArthur escaped Corregidor for Australia, leaving the seventy-six thousand sick and starving American and Filipino defenders. In Corregidor, the thirteen thousand survivors surrendered on May 6, 1942, and on May 9, 1942, there were seventy-six thousand sick and starving American and Filipino defenders surrendered in Bataan. While they were forced to undergo the brutal Bataan Death March, there were seven thousand to ten thousand who died or viciously murdered. The Japanese put many Filipinos into hard labor, and many young Filipino women were made to provide sex services. For three years, the Filipinos suffered in the hands of Japanese imperial government while remaining hopeful for General MacArthur's return and America's promise of independence; that made the Filipinos remain loyal to the United States. On October 20, 1944, General MacArthur fulfilled his promise, the "I shall return," and landed on the island of Leyte with his forces of seven hundred vessels and 174,000 men. The islands of Mindoro and Leyte were cleared of Japanese invaders, while Manila and other cities turned into ruins, and millions of Filipinos died side by side the Americans when the Japanese attempted to defend and maintained control of the land.[35]

The Japanese came and forcefully ruled over the Philippines. When the Japanese succeeded in occupying the entire country, they started maltreating human lives. They persecuted the Filipinos, raped their women, took their properties, and killed whoever is against them. They controlled the media to suppress freedom of speech. They required all citizens and houses with radios to be registered, or else, their houses get raided, and they would be thrown to Fort Santiago and for "water cure" torture. There was a time that the tortured victims' suffered punishments by hanging the bodies of guerrilla suspects and beat them with four by four piece of wood, pressing with a red-hot iron or electric wire into their flesh and at the end beheaded them.

Under the Japanese rule, the Filipinos were not only scared of the Japanese military and Japanese Filipino spies, but they also suffered diseases and hunger. They had sleepless nights waiting to get arrested and tortured. They were afraid of to walk down the streets as they were not sure what would happen next. With less powered weapons, the Filipino guerrilla fought against the Japanese colonizers. They went to the mountains and tried to form forces against the Japanese, but it was just impossible for them to defeat the Japanese with high-powered weapons.[36]

The Japanese control in the Philippines ended when the United States unleashed the deadly atomic bomb in Hiroshima, demolishing almost half of the city and killing thousands of inhabitants.[37] Again, the Philippines were taken back by the Americans from the control of imperial Japan.

The different successive colonial form of government caused the natives Filipinos developed the mixed attitude toward foreign colonizers and the struggle for reform has been the desire of many generations that made some Filipinos vulnerable to new ideologies

E. **The Philippine Independence**

In 1946, after more than three hundred years under foreign rules, the Philippines gained its independence and became a democratic republic. At this time, the Filipino people were given the freedom to rule over their country. The Philippines became independent, and Manuel Roxas became president.[38] Since then, the Filipino American friendship strongly developed. After Pres. Manuel Roxas, six presidents were elected in succession until Pres. Ferdinand E. Marcos got elected in 1965.

F. The 1972 Martial Law – The Marcos Regime

Toward the end of President Marcos's second term, he declared martial law on September 21, 1972, suspending democratic institutions, restricting civil rights, and arresting political opponents. He took control of the media and imprisoned whoever was politically against him, but after twenty years in power, he declared a snap election to test his popularity and leadership. The widow of the slain Benigno Aquino Jr., Corazon C. Aquino, stood up to run against him. In the midst of widespread election fraud reports, Marcos claimed to be the winner, but a four-day protest in Manila known as EDSA People Power movement led by a Roman Catholic Cardinal Sin toppled the Marcos regime in February 1986. An aircraft lifted the Marcos family from Malacañang and brought them to Hawaii. A new lady president, Corazon C. Aquino, succeeded in power and promulgated a new constitution based on democratic principles ratified in the following year. The Philippines, at this time, shaped its place in the newly industrialized nation of Asia and sought greater integration in the region while it's colonial past remained in the hearts and minds of those who were afflicted. The facts above clearly tell us that the Filipinos suffered extreme discontentment and maltreatments from their colonizers, even by its leaders in power, for more than three hundred years. During those years, their pains and grievances had been suppressed. There were few who rose and fought to gain their freedom from tyranny, yet they fought powerlessly not until the EDSA People Power revolt arose.

The next chapter focuses on how these pains and grievances, which some Filipinos felt for a very long time, led to ant colonialism, how abuse and maltreatment molded the Filipinos to being too much on guard on their rights, having a questioning and not too trusting attitude toward those who are in power.

CHAPTER 3

The Progression of Filipino Anti-Colonialism

BEFORE THE SPANIARDS arrived in the Philippines, the Filipinos had no idea about being a country. However, they had already developed relationships with China, Malaysia, and other neighboring Asian nations. The excruciating experiences of the Filipinos with the Spanish intruders marked the beginning of Filipino consciousness about nationalism, and they became a nation of their identity driven by their desire for an independent government led by Filipinos after painful experiences of colonial abuses and maltreatment. No doubt that the Philippines had already developed trade relationship with Chinese and other Malayan traders before the Spaniards came to the Philippines. The Filipino culture was enriched by neighboring Asian countries even before the last three colonizers arrived and took part in the development of grievances or anti-colonialism among Filipinos; the Spaniards, Americans, and Japanese treated them with prejudice and instilled it in the minds of the old folks. Because of the extreme abuse during colonization, the old veterans had developed grievances or rebellious attitude toward the European or Western colonizers. They have personal testimonies, stories, memories, and experiences of people who had gone through this regime and who are alive and suffering from physical and psychological wounds and trauma.

These untold stories help us understand the causes and the process why rebellion and terrorism developed in the character of some Filipinos, particularly the old folks and Muslim communities. The Spanish religious intolerance for those who would not submit to the

Roman church created religious prejudice that led to resistance against the Spaniards. The Spaniards hired spies and captured unconverted, resistant native religious priests or leaders and killed them. The Spaniards used Filipinos to kill other Filipinos and had them mercilessly stuck, fastened their dead bodies on a bamboo, and placed in the river to be eaten by crocodiles.[39] There were several factors that influenced the attitude of the freedom-loving Filipinos. During the Spaniards' regime, they introduced reforms but overwhelmed by abuses, oppression, and greediness of wealth and power, which developed hatred among Filipinos. It led to more than one hundred patchy revolts and rebellion from different regions in the country against the Spaniards. Filipinos desired to regain their lost freedom and hated paying tribute, doing forced labor, victims of land grabbing, and economic reasons. The Spanish friars owning or taking the big portion of lands and properties to enrich themselves, while the Filipino farmers had none or only a limited land to till for a living.[40]

Before the Spaniards arrived, the entire Mindanao was previously occupied by the Native Filipinos and Muslim tribe. The first Spanish expedition to Mindanao, with Roman Catholic Church expansion to Muslim communities, caused Muslim resistance. The Spaniards wanted more of what they had and attacked Mindanao to put all islands under their control. They first attacked the island of Jolt; the Muslims settlers were defeated but unconquered. The Muslims then declared war against the Spaniards. Later, the Spaniards moved to attack Cotabato and other provinces, but again, the Spaniards failed to defeat Maguindanao Muslims and, worse, Spanish Captain Figueroa died in battle.

Knowing that some Visayan Christians helped the Spaniards fight them, grievances against the Spaniards and Visayan Christian settlers created hatred and tension that led the Muslims to attack the Visayan islands of Cebu, Negros, and Panay. The Muslim attackers were called Juramentados.[41]

CHAPTER 4

The Birth of Philippine Nationalism

DESPITE OF COURAGEOUS defense of their land, the Filipino revolts failed because of lack of national leaders and spirit of nationalism. Although they have shown bravery and strong determination, they were weakened by the Spanish "divide it impera" (divide and rule), a strategy created to divide and conquer. The idea of nationalism was truly foreign to the Filipinos until the executions of the three priests—Father Gomez, Father Burgos, and Father Zamora (GOMBURZA)—and Dr. Jose Rizal. The lack of national leaders caused disunity among Filipinos, but the spirit of nationalism emerged out of many unsuccessful Filipino revolts against the Spaniards that made them realize the importance of national leadership, nationalism, and unity.[42] The Filipinos were determined to have their freedom and took courage to stand up against the Spaniards.

Long before the Spaniards came, the natives in the Philippines already had some cultural heritage, love of freedom, and common ancestral religion. They already had trading businesses with other Asian countries, but the natives had no idea about one supreme government for an entire archipelago. When the Spanish colonizers arrived, they had added a Roman religion and set up a centralized government.

Although there was so much negativism under the Spanish government, no one could deny that the Spaniards also had good contributions and made positive impact to the country. One of it was the growth of nationalism, culture, and the opening of the World Trade 1834 that allowed the flow of different imported and exported products from Europe and Asia to the Philippines and vice versa. They did not only import/export good quality products but also brought in with them books, magazines, and good new ideas regarding the democratic system of governance, ideas of freedom, of equality and human rights, which opened the eyes of the natives for good and fair governance and to identify abuses in government. The low cost of transportation going to Europe encouraged middle-class families to send their kids to Europe to study, and there they learned the ideas of nationalism, human rights, and liberalism that helped them understand the civilized democratic government which they never enjoyed in their country Their education introduced to them new ideas, and they started feeling being abused, exploited, and deprived of opportunities.[43]

At the height of grievances, a group of leading Filipino reformists, which included Dr. Jose Rizal, Marcelo H. Del Pilar, Graciano Lopez Jaena, Juan Luna, Pedro Paterno, Mariano Ponce, Jose Panganiban, Ma. Regidor, and Isabelo De Los Reyes, organized the *La Solidaridad*, the official newspaper of the Propaganda Movement. It aimed to create an effective campaign for reforms at the height of the Filipino grievances against the ruling Spaniards. The contributors were Filipino intellectuals who went to study and live in Spain. They used pen names to hide their identity in criticizing Spanish friars and government officials. Because of strict censorship, the paper was distributed in secret, and some copies were passed on to Filipinos who smuggled it into the Philippines. It became an eye-opener to the real conditions of the country. Through it, they were able to express their resentment and grievances against the Spanish regime. Because of lack of funds, the Propaganda Movement declined. When Dr. Jose Rizal returned to the Philippines in 1892, he organized another movement, La Liga Filipina, to continue his peaceful campaign for reforms. Despite of the existence of the Propaganda Movement, the Spanish officials continued with their abusive and unjust acts against the Filipinos. After four days, Rizal was arrested and exiled to Dapitan, Mindanao, awaiting his sentence. Later, he was sentenced to death at the Luneta Park. Dr. Jose Rizal then became a national hero for facing his death rather than recanting his writings against Spanish abuses and injustices. Nevertheless, the Propaganda Movement contributed to the development of nationalism among Filipinos.

Dr. Jose Rizal also wrote two books, *Noli Me Tangere* and *El Filibusterismo*, that were distributed in secret. The books exposed the Spaniards' abuses against women, among others, hoping that the king or queen of Spain would be able to discover the maltreatments and abuses against the Filipinos by Spanish friars or rulers. But again, because of lack of funds and unity in the group, the Propaganda Movement declined. The movement asked for the abolition of tribute, reduction of forced labor from forty days a year to fifteen days, creation of civil provinces under a civil governor, reforms in the local government, and the abolition of tobacco monopoly.

Since then, Rizal's heroic life and the lives of other national heroes became models to young Filipinos. The study of Rizal's life and his writings is included only in public schools' curriculum but not offered in Roman Catholic universities and colleges, trying to conceal the records of the Spanish friars' abuses and maltreatments to Filipinos.

Philippine history turned out so brief and simplified, if not modified. History books written by Western historians do not reveal the complete story of the country. Many unanswered questions in the last colonial wars remain hidden in the next generation.

CHAPTER 5

The Anti-Colonialism Exasperation

THIS PART OF the book will help us identify the source of Filipino anticolonialism spirit. This will explain what aggravated the Filipinos to when it comes to issues about suppression of rights and maltreatment and how it became easy for them to resort to rebellion.

This author could still remember his grandfather holding him on his lap while being told of his experiences during the Spanish and Japanese regimes. As a guerilla during the time of the Spaniards until the Japanese imperial government, he hid in the mountains and changed his name for the security of his family. He was one of those unfortunate Filipinos who experienced terrible abuse from the colonizers. Looking at his face, I listened as he narrated that how he hid in the jungle, not knowing that the war had already ended. He came down to town in the early 1950s, only when he heard that the Japanese had already pulled out from the country and the war was totally over. While hiding in the mountains, his name was not even listed as a member of USAFE when the US Armed forces collected the names of Filipino soldiers or guerrillas after the war to include them in the rosters of the US veterans armed in the Philippines.

While recollecting his experiences and the gruesome incidents, his grandchildren listened; this author was sitting on his lap. He talked about his personal experiences with gnashing teeth and anger against the colonizers. He recalled that there were still unrecorded massacre and gruesome incidents that the Philippine historians missed to document.

He described how the Japanese threw babies into the air and positioned a sharp bayonet where they would drop. He saw how young and minor women were taken from schools and returned home with tears in their eyes after being abused during Spanish and Japanese regimes. He could still imagine how families survived living in fear of getting randomly picked up. There were individuals whose whereabouts are unknown until now, missing or forgotten. With a loud shaking voice, he told heartbreaking detailed stories of incidents unreported and unrecorded, except maybe in his memory. My grandfather died at 128 year old.

The Philippine Consulate General Website in Sydney confirmed this historical record about the Spaniards' harsh treatment of the Filipino people in many areas of the country during their three-century rule. The imposition of heavy taxation, mandatory service or hard labor hurt especially the peasant class. It resulted in sporadic revolts throughout the archipelago, but generally, these were severely dealt with and controlled by the Spaniards.[44] The unwritten stories of pain and struggle were retained in the minds of the people and marked with tears and blood of innocents and powerless citizens. Some big old churches made of bricks and stones erected during Spanish time still exist today and may remind us of the hard labor and sufferings of force labor of the enslaved Filipinos.

According to Tali Miriam Master, in her dissertation, "The Link Between Moral Anger and Social Activism: An Explorative Study," when a person experience injustices, he may develop anger, hatred, and bitterness. He may become so aggressive when it comes to activism. Her study explores one of the pathways to creating change, via examining the mechanism that allows some individuals who have experienced anger as a result of growing up under a system. Her study explains the reason the present attitudes of the Filipinos of being so attached to the ideology of fighting for their rights in a violent way. When feelings of anger and hatred suppressed for many years provoked them to create and organize resistant groups. It's always been their last resort to fight for what they believed in or revenge for the injustices they suffered.[45]

Andres Bonifacio, one of the Philippines's national heroes, expressed his thoughts and feelings about the Spaniards' abuses and compared these to a mother who neglects her children. In a time when media was controlled and the freedom of expression was suppressed, Andres Bonifacio, found ways to communicate to his fellow Filipinos through the poems he wrote. Through his writings, he described his feelings of pain, anger, and hatred toward the Spaniards for their maltreatment of the Filipinos; he related the hardships of the Filipinos under the Spanish colonial rule. The abusive rule and maltreatment painfully marked into the hearts and minds of the Filipinos and caused hatred and grievances to develop. It led them to rise against their colonial oppressor. It created an antagonistic and rebellious attitude toward foreigners and encouraged them to form and lead different groups. The author of an article quoted Andres Bonifacio who compared Spain to a mother who neglects her children:

> *"Spain hurts his child, the Philippines, through brutal treatment, instead of nurturing her. In the process, Spain released an unmistakable wrath from her children . . . he warned Spain that the end of its cruelty to the Philippines is nearing . . . because of suffering it had to endure for so long, the child rise against it".*[46]

The series of wars, grievances against colonizers, maltreatments, successive corrupt officials, and unrecorded brutalities in the history of the Philippines preconditioned the minds of Filipinos to rebellion, communism, insurgency, and terrorism. Unless they achieve a true democratic government, dreams and hope for reforms remain unrealized. Thus, rebellion or joining a terrorist group has been their last recourse for change. As a result of previous events, the Philippines became the breeding ground for splits of Al-Qaeda-linked groups organized and formed by warlike people who need public recognition, exploited by politicians at the expense of innocent lives, peace and order, and economic development.

Martha Crenshaw pointed out in her research,

> *"The first condition that can be considered a direct cause of terrorism is the existence of concrete grievances among an identifiable subgroup of a larger population, such as an ethnic minority discriminated against by the majority. A social movement develops in order to redress these grievances and to gain either equal rights or a separate state; terrorism is then the resort of an extremist faction of this broader movement . . ."*[47]

The long years of Filipino suffering from their colonizers created grievances and hatred in them. These things preconditioned the minds of Filipinos to become vulnerable to anti-colonialism and be prepared to accept terroristic ideologies. The pain and suffering of the Filipinos from their colonizers and the suppression they encountered from tyrant rulers aggravated their anger, and it led them to create resistant groups and later linked to Al-Qaeda and developed them to become aggressive terrorists.

CHAPTER 6

The Rise of Terrorist Groups

THE COMPLICATED ATTITUDE of many Filipinos toward foreign colonizers and the struggle for reform has been the dream of all generations. They became susceptible to new ideologies that prompted them to the formation of radical, rebellious, or terroristic groups.

A. *The Origin of the Hukbalahap or Huks*

From 1946 to 1952, the Philippine government struggled against a tenacious enemy, the Hukbalahap or Huk; the abbreviation was derived from the Tagalog name of the group, Hukbo ng Bayan Laban sa Hapon. It was a guerrilla army formed during the Japanese occupation in 1941–1945. Many guerrillas fought during WWII against the Japanese army, and some even managed to escape or survived the Bataan Death March. However, when the Japanese surrendered in 1945, the Huks diverted their fight for the rights of the Filipino tenant farmers against the rich and wealthy land owners.

Luis Taruc, the guerrilla leader, gallantly fought against the Japanese and regained most provinces of Luzon from the imperial Japanese army and left an impressive legacy. Taruc ran for Congress in 1946. He got elected but was unable to seat on charges of fraud and terrorism. He went to the mountains with his followers, and they called their group the Peoples Liberation Army (PLA). He planned to set up a communist government. From the poor peasants exploited by the landlords, he recruited a new guerrilla army and set himself as president.

In 1949, PLA members ambushed and killed Aurora Quezon, the widow of former Philippine president Manuel Quezon. She was shot dead along with her eldest daughter and son-in-law. Aurora Quezon was the head of the Philippine Red Cross. She was known for her humanitarian works and kindness that many potential recruits were discouraged to join and eventually turned against the PLA. Many wealthy landowners across Luzon, with a strong connection to the government in Manila, were killed. PLA was considered a left-wing organization, and although not closely associated with the Communist Party of the Philippines, the United States offered assistance to the newly independent government to provide military advisers to the Philippine government in anti-PLA operations. In 1954, Luis Taruc surrendered through negotiation and the effort of a young Sen. Benigno "Ninoy" Aquino Jr., and did not resist serving a prison sentence.[48]

B. *The Rise of the New People's Army (NPA)*

Insurgency and rebellion in the Philippines could be traced back to "peasants" rebellions in the nineteenth century up to the twentieth century. Rural peasants revolted because of land tenancy and agrarian issues in the 1950s, which made them inclined or became susceptible to communist ideology. The agrarian problems were carried down to the next generations, and the Partido Komunista ng Pilipinas (PKP), a communist party, had inherited the agrarian issues from the Spanish Regime. The PKP was established in the 1930s, along with the Hukbalahap war guerillas. Rebellion declined in the 1950s, but the remaining Huk members were instrumental in forming the New People's Army (NPA), linked to Chinese communism of Mao Zedong modeled with its Agrarian revolution. Because of ideological differences and rivalries in party leadership, Jose Maria Sison, with educated middle- class youth and other young revolutionaries in Central Luzon who were disgruntled by the government, founded the Communist Party of the Philippines (CPP) in 1968 during the second term of Pres. Ferdinand Marcos. The group criticized the Marcos government policy with the United States and regarded armed revolution as the only way to overthrow their alleged US-sponsored Philippine government. The CPP ideology sought to address the following issues: reform in agrarian and land tenancy system; poor economic conditions and unemployment, including inequitable income distribution; and the lack of government credibility because of abuses and corruption. The CPP promoted a peasant-led revolution, but the group lacked peasant base and had no knowledge of "guerilla warfare." Eventually, the CPP made an ally with Bernabe Buscayno, known as Kumander Dante, who was directly involved in previous peasant guerilla activities in the 1960s emerging from PKH-Huk. Buscayno submitted and came under the leadership of the CPP and formed the CPP-New People's Army. To advance their causes, the CPP-NPA engaged in extortion, revolutionary taxes, and bombings of important targets.[49]

The CPP-NPA operation converged on agrarian reform against the inherited agrarian system patterned from the Spanish friars' land-grabbing syndicate during the Spanish regime. The idea made the rural peasants susceptible to this cause.

C. *The Operation Merdika*

The Marcos regime initiated the Operation Merdeka, the code name used by the military involved in the recruitment of about two hundred young Tausug and Samal Muslims, aged eighteen to thirty, from Sulu and Tawi-Tawi. They were trained at Simunul Island, where the first Arab missionary Makhdum built a mosque for the first time in the fourteenth century. The recruiters promised the young recruits with benefits, not only monthly allowance but also guns, which they considered very precious, and the opportunity to become part of the military elite in the armed forces. Their commando unit trained in Simunul Island called Jabidah.

On December 30, 1968, after the training in Simunul, they were transported to the island of Corregidor in Northern Luzon on board a Philippine Navy vessel for the second phase of their specialized training program. But later, the young recruits became disgruntled after they discovered the real purpose of their training and mission. The plan was not only to invade Sabah but also to kill their Muslim relatives living there. They were also disappointed and frustrated because of the nonpayment of their Ph50.00 monthly allowance as promised. Thus, they refused to obey orders and demanded to return home. Their military officials, together with the people who were behind the said mission, had only one option left to settle the mess, and that was to kill them all. Thus, the Jabidah Massacre happened.

Jubin Arula, the sole survivor, revealed that at night of March 18, 1968, the trainees were led outside the Corregidor barracks in groups of twelve. After a while, he heard a series of gunshots and saw his colleagues fell and none was able to call "Alla" or "Mama." Fortunately, he was able to escape through the mountains and rolled off the cliff toward the sea. He clung to a floating piece of wood until morning and, fortunately, was rescued by a Cavite fisherman.

The Philippine media or press bombarded Malacañang with criticism, attacking so much against Marcos Regime rather than the soldiers involved.

In 1970, the case even elevated its way to the Supreme Court but still on a preliminary status. The Muslims, claiming that at least twenty-eight Moro army recruits were murdered, did a weeklong vigil protest with an empty coffin marked "Jabidah" staged in front of Malacañang. The twenty-three accused military personnel were court-martialed, even up to the Supreme Court, but nothing could stand against an invincible Marcos regime. The Jabidah incident led to the formation of the Moro National Liberation Front (MNLF).[50]

D. *Jabidah Massacre led to the Formation of MNLF.*

On Corregidor Island, made the Muslim community indignant and released their contained anger from years of prejudice, ill-treatment, and discrimination. Muslim students conducted a weeklong widespread protest vigil with an empty coffin marked "Jabidah" placed in front of Malacañang Palace. Founded on hatred and resentment, the MNLF was conceptualized and formed as a result of the "Jabidah Massacre." The Jabidah training mission was an attempt of Pres. Ferdinand E. Marcos to claim Sabah, as it originally belongs to the sultan of Sulu. But primarily, he was more interested in raising a private army for his political interests, and the loophole in Jabidah Massacre led to the existence of National Liberation Front (NLF). The phrase "National Liberation Front" was taken and inspired from the National Liberation Movement of South Vietnam in the 1960s. Having exposed to Marxism-Leninist-Maoist radicalism and as a professor at the University of the Philippines, Nur Misuari was involved with the radical Kabataang Makabayan (KM), a student activist group, and its communist founding leader, Jose Maria Sison, aligned by their same secular nationalist orientation, influenced his activism to Moro nationalism. Must he have some influence on the ideological perception of the students? The first vice chairman, Abul Khayr Alonto, added the word "Moro" to complete the group's name, Moro National Liberation Front (MNLF). Its goal is to reclaim Muslim Mindanao, Sulu, and Palawan (MINSUPALA). Abul Khayr Alonto and Jallaludin Santos, with Muslim congressmen and leaders who were at that time active with the Bangsamoro movement, recruited young men from different Muslim tribes. Both Alonto and Santos conceptualized and organized MNLF with the idea that they could benefit from Nur Misuari's intelligence and influence with the leftist group Kabataang Barangay (KM). They persuaded Misuari to join the movement. Alonto declined to chair MNLF and suggested that Misuari should be the chairman of MNLF and he was in the best position to articulate or represent the group in the international community involving Bangsamoro problems. In 1973-1975, with the support of Libya and Malaysia, the MNLF's claim for Mindanao independence escalated to its peak. The MNLF fielded about thirty thousand armed fighters against the military, about 70-80 percent of its combat forces, which resulted to an estimate of fifty thousand casualties.[51]

E. *The Abu Sayyaf – A Group of Bandits*

In 1990, the Abu Sayyaf Group was formed with the assistance of Al Qaeda's founder, Osama Bin Laden. Basilan Island in Sulu became their stronghold. The island was populated with about four hundred thousand people. Aside from the support of Osama Bin Laden, the Abu Sayyaf engages in kidnap-for-ransom operations and demands huge amount in exchange of their captive's freedom. The kidnap victims are released only upon payment of their ransom. Some were killed for noncompliance to their demands.[52]

Gracia Burnham, after a year of captivity, recalled,

> *"After a year you get to know those guys and you get to hear their stories. And you hear how they're not really bent on jihad. A lot of those guys were young guys and they wanted to get married and in that culture it's the guy who pays the bride price. The*

economy in that part of the country is horrible. So if your father is a poor fisherman, where are you going to get 50,000 pesos to buy a bride? So they would join the Abu Sayyaf almost as a career move and hope they were there when somebody paid the ransom so they could go home and get married. When you hear those stories . . . your heart can't help but go out to them. A lot of them didn't want to be there".[53]

These guys have different reasons why they joined the Abu Sayyaf.

F.   *The Peace Treaty Agreements*

In 1976, Nur Misuari, with the Philippine government, signed the Tripoli Peace Agreement during the Marcos regime and eventually became the first governor of the Autonomous Region of Muslim Mindanao (ARMM). During the Ramos administration, however, a new group, the Moro Islamic Liberation Front (MILF), broke away from MNLF and continued the fight against the government. They did not agree with the peace treaty between Misuari and the Philippine government and persistently struggled against the Philippine government. There were hundreds of lives lost and still, there's no peace in the region.

On March 27, 2014, the Philippine government, under Pres. Ninoy Aquino's administration, and the MILF signed another peace treaty called the Comprehensive Agreement on the Bangsamoro, replacing the Autonomous Region in Muslim Mindanao, while Nur Misuari's influence was declining and may have been losing more supporters because of the split with the MILF. Misuari's nine-year rule of the ARMM endured with deafening complaints from local officials about mismanagement and loss of confidence on Nur Misuari's leadership.[54]

Unfortunately, the signing angered Nur Misuari, believing that it violated the rights of the MNLF and the 1996 peace deal. At Talipao, Sulu, he proclaimed the Bangsamoro Republic independence on August 12, 2013,[55] yet he was ignored by the Philippine government, and he was seldom heard in the media.

In September 9, 2013, Misuari was enraged by the Philippine government by signing another peace treaty with the MILF for the Bangsamoro autonomy in Mindanao. The MNLF founding chairman,

Nur Misuari, with his armed men attacked Zamboanga City, which caused millions' worth of property damage and cost hundreds of innocent lives. At the height of the attacks, Misuari launched against the heavy forces of the military and ended up with twenty hostages.[56] They failed to conquer Zamboanga City, and when the armed MNLF men had nowhere to escape, again, they wanted a peace talk, "Quraysh," a revolutionary tactic of Mohammed.

Over the radio interviews by the media, MNLF spokesman, Atty. Emmanuel Fontanilla, demanded an immediate "cease fire." Atty. Fontanilla called for the United Nations and international community to intervene or mediate for their demands. Misuari accused the Philippine government of ignoring and violating the Tripoli Agreement he signed with the MNLF by recognizing and signing another peace treaty with the MILF.

G. *The Formation of MILF – Funded by Muammar Gaddafi*

The Moro Islamic Liberation Front (MILF) was formed by Hashim Salamat after he split from the Moro National Islamic Front (MNLF); the later was advocating a reconciliatory move toward the government. Chairman Nur Misuari of the MNLF signed an agreement in January 1987 with the Philippine government. He accepted the offer of Muslim autonomy in exchange for relinquishing its goal of independence for Muslim Mindanao. Hashim Salamat disagreed to Nur Misuari's move, and with the support of the ethnic group Maguindanao, Hashim Salamat organized the MILF with around three thousand armed members in the field split from the MNLF. But recently, under Pres. Benigno Aquino's administration, the MILF signed a peace treaty with the Philippine government, advocating moderate and reconciliatory gesture toward the government and eventually accepted the offer of Muslim autonomy rather than their claim of independence for Muslim Mindanao. Hashim Salamat agreed and accepted the government's offer for Muslim Autonomy the same idea that he disagreed with Nur Misuari.

It is evident that these terrorist groups were formed by leaders who split, join, and form another group with influential members, like what Hashim Salamat did. He was a member of the MNLF but later withdrew and created the MILF. The claim for Muslim Mindanao independence has always been the reason for creating a rebel group and an issue against the government. Forming another group is very common for the warlike Muslim people with enough courage and leadership. They established their group for possible huge monetary consideration to support their cause from the Middle East. According to the report of the Moro leaders themselves, Muammar Gaddafi of Libya financially supported the creation of both the MNLF and MILF.[57] The facts in this chapter also show that most members of these rebel groups are Muslim constituents of the Philippines that when traced back to history were also the same Filipino Muslim race who aggressively fought against the Philippine colonizers. Even when Manila surrendered, they never did but continue the fight until today.

H. *Bangsamoro Islamic Freedom Fighter (BIFF)*

In 2013, another Muslim group, the Bangsamoro Islamic Freedom Fighters (BIFF), emerged when Pres. Benigno Aquino III ignored the Tripoli Agreement with the MNLF and signed another peace treaty with MILF while both parties were at the negotiating table. This newly organized group was formed under the leadership of Uztadz Ameril Umbra Kato, a Saudi Arabia-trained scholar and a former MILF leader. For the same reason, when Hashim Salamat left the MNLF, Kato reacted to the MILF's more compromising and accommodating gesture toward the government. He left MILF and formed another group, the BIFF. He took the baton of leadership demanding for Mindanao independence.[58] Kato and Salamat both defected from the MNLF when Misuari accepted the offer of Mindanao autonomy in place of Muslim Mindanao independence. Now later, Kato, the leader of the new group, BIFF, declared disagreement to the MILF's peace treaty with the Philippine government and sought for national and international recognition. It's a strategy to gain possible monetary support. At this point, there'll be no end of creating new rebel or terrorist groups when the previous group signed a peace treaty with the government for its leaders' possible political interest, personal privileges, and interest from the government in lieu of their claim for Muslim Mindanao Independence. Later, the MILF was trying to convince the Philippine Senate to approve the proposed Bangsamoro Basic Law (BBL) that they would be allowed to have their independent government, which is tantamount to allowing them to have a state within the state with a demand of a big chunk of money that the national government should allocate for the BBL. The 117 billion pesos for BBL implementation only require approval from Congress, but the bill did not pass in the Senate.[59] The amount looks very attractive to the Muslim leaders, but as it is unconstitutional, it did not pass in the Senate. While in the process, the BIFF is now silent and observant, waiting for their turn to continue the fight for Muslim Mindanao independence and do the same.

It's sad to note that this claim for Muslim Mindanao independence never ends. The result of the forthcoming presidential election on May 9, 2016, would determine the future of the proposed BBL. One of the presidential candidate's political platforms promised to change the Philippine government from a corrupt centralized form to a federal system. The huge crowds in all the campaign rallies of Duterte demonstrate the demand for real change. The mayor of Davao City, Atty. Rodrigo Duterte, said, like the Muslim people in Mindanao, he had similar sad experience with the centralized government in Manila. He was criticized for his bad mouth and cursing, but in his discourse he said that in every cursing he uttered, there is a sad story of every Filipino behind it. He wanted to establish a government for the people. Duterte said, he would listen to the cry of all tribes and races in the country and try to consolidate the BBL in the federal system of government he wants to establish for the Philippines. Now let's wait for real change to come and hope for the best!

CHAPTER 7

The Root Cause of Continuous Rebellion and Terrorism in the Philippines

IN READING ABOUT the origin or real cause of war and political conflicts, some biblical research and writings relevant to the issue provided an answer why men, even nations, go to wars.

1. The Greed of Money, Fame, and Power.

Atul Joshi, wrote a short essay about the love of money saying;

> *"Love of money," it is said, " is the root of half the evil in the world; lack of money the root of the other half." Both these statements are broadly true. The implications of the first statement are obvious enough the love and lure of wealth prompt people to resort to all sorts of malpractices, such as hoarding, black market, deception, miserliness, greed, and dishonesty . . . When pockets a cherished more than hearts and brains, human bodies, justice, and dignity? And deterioration of character and morals sets in, gradually but surely. The love and possession of wealth also bring in their wake callousness and dislike of the weak and lack of sympathy towards the helpless."[60]*

In addition to that, a published message in "God and Truth website" pointed out the reason why the world is in chaos and turmoil is the pervasive desire for power, status, fame, and recognition. The article says,

"The corridors of history are littered with much destruction, pain and suffering because of the unrestrained lust for power and glory. Often, this lust goes together with abuse of power, corruption and greed for material gains. This can take place among small groups of people as well as in whole nations embroiled in bitter conflicts and devastating wars. These hostilities and clashes may arise from the ambitions of a few dictators and their followers. Thousands and millions suffer and die because of the tyrannical rule and the whims and fancies of these leaders. In many countries, there seems to be unending political and social instability due to constant jostling for power and all kinds of political intrigues."[61]

The above statements are supported by the Holy Scripture, the Bible, when St. Paul told his disciple Timothy,

"For the love of money is the root of all evil: which while some coveted after, they have erred from the faith, and pierced themselves through with many sorrows."[62]

In another portion of the scripture, St. James, in his epistle to the twelve tribes scattered abroad, said,

"What causes quarrels and what causes fights among you? Is it not this, that your passions are at war within you? You desire and do not have, so you murder. You covet and cannot obtain, so you fight and quarrel . . ."[63]

Therefore, selfishness; greed of wealth and money; desire for fame, honor, and power are the causes of conflicts and wars among men and even nations in the world. With it, there would be no peace among humanity and on earth.

A. *The Exploitation of Rebellion and Terrorism for Political Interests*

During the regime of Pres. Ferdinand Marcos, he envisioned to invade Sabah, Malaysia, being claimed as historically part of the Philippines. Before he proclaimed martial law, he orchestrated the special military training of young Muslim Tausug men, with a promise of monetary allowance while on training, weapons, and elite military membership. After their training, when the military officers were about to send them out to their mission, they were told that their mission was to invade Sabah. The group was disgruntled when the military officers failed to give their promised allowance while on training. They refused to obey and wanted to go home. Then the Jabidah Massacre happened. Despite of the Marcos-controlled media, this information leaked out. This story began in 1968, when a twenty-seven-year-old Jibin Arula and several Moro youths were recruited by military officers during the Marcos regime for a top-secret mission called "Operation Merdeka" (Operation Freedom). Their mission was to destabilize, invade, and grab Sabah from Malaysia. Jabidah was the name of their first training camp in 1967 in Simunul Island, located at last group of islands facing Sabah, Malaysia, which is still considered part of Sulu. Arula, the lone survivor, who revealed the information about the Jabidah Massacre incident, recently died just in an accident after hiding for many years.[64]

B. *Insurrection and Rebellion - Pretext for Martial Law Declaration*

Whether the claim of the sultanate of Sulu and the Philippine government over Sabah, Malaysia, is legitimate or not, the creation of "fear and terror" was a smart initiative to create the existence of invasion, rebellion, and insurgency in the country. The Marcos Operation Merdeka, which resulted to Jabidah Massacre, could have drawn "invasion" on either side of Malaysia or Philippines, which may establish a ground for war and declaration of martial law. It would not only be a good pretext for the declaration of martial law, but it could also extend Ferdinand Marcos's stay in power. It had been a common talk of many that Pres. Ferdinand E. Marcos judiciously used the law for his political advantage when he declared martial law in the Philippines. Article 7, Section 11, # 2 of the Philippine Constitution provides that

"The President shall be commander-in-chief of all armed forces of the Philippines and, whenever it becomes necessary, he may call out such armed forces to prevent or suppress lawless violence, invasion, insurrection, or rebellion. In case of invasion, insurrection, rebellion, or imminent danger thereof, when the public safety requires it; he may suspend the privileges of the writ of habeas corpus, or place the Philippines or part thereof under martial law."[65]

This article provided no time limit on how long the government under martial law regime would last. As the provision left no time limit for martial rule, it's up to the discretion of the commander in chief. The constitution only stated that "in case of invasion, insurrection, rebellion, or imminent danger thereof, when the public safety requires it . . ." There's no time limit. Therefore, the continuous existence of terror, rebellion, insurrection, invasion, and violence may be enough reason to place the entire country under martial rule.

President Marcos, with Juan Ponce Enrile, his secretary of defense at that time, took advantage of that loophole in the provision. From my student and teenage years, lots of speeches and remarks were personally heard and read from some news reporters and political opponents accusing the Marcos regime and confirming Marcos' manipulative use of martial law provision just to extend his stay in power. The Marcos regime was suspected of possible sabotaging and faking rebellion, bombings, and particularly the ambush of Sec. Juan Ponce Enrile, which became one of the major reasons of the martial law declaration in September 21, 1972.[66] The twenty years of Marcos regime did not stand without opposition, which demanded for the lifting of martial rule that cost the lives and imprisonment of some political opponents, missing individuals even accused the Marcos Regime of killing his number one political rival Sen. Benigno Aquino upon his arrival at Manila International Airport. Benigno Aquino insisted on returning to the Philippines from exile in the United States despite of Marcos's disapproval. Upon his arrival at the Manila International Airport, he was shot and killed. After the incident, Marcos spoke through the media and charged the crime to the terrorists, implicating the suspected assassin as member of the communist party.[67]

Despite of the alleged powerful cover-up, the late Senator Diokno, with other Marcos's political opposition, continuously questioned the declaration of martial law and suspected the uniformed personnel who picked up Aquino from the plane did the plot to kill him with the blessing of higher authority. Senator Diokno and his group traveled throughout the country to conduct rallies and accused the Marcos government as responsible for the death of Aquino. He accused Marcos of creating an atmosphere of fear and terror and preserved the presence of terrorism and rebellion to sustain the need of martial rule. Sen. Ceasar Climaco from Zamboanga City claimed never to cut his already very long hair unless Mr. Marcos lifted his martial rule. Climaco was silenced only by a single shot in the head and died with a very long hair.

During Pres. Gloria M. Arroyo's administration, Sen. Aquilino Pimentel and Sen. Juan Ponce Enrile, during a Senate session, did have an intense personal argument televised on ABS-CBN news. While watching their debate, Enrile accused Pimentel of being a coward, but Pimentel responded and defended himself and recalled being imprisoned during the Marcos regime, with Juan Ponce Enrile as the minister of national defense, to prove his courage and bravery. Pimentel accused Enrile of sabotaging and faking his own ambush to justify Marcos's declaration of martial law. Senator Enrile did not respond to the issue and sat down in silence. His demeanor may have proven it was true. Having a glimpse of the Marcos crucial time when the defense minister of Marcos government Juan Ponce Enrile together with Gen. Fidel Ramos had a failed coup against Marcos. Later, the news was about Marcos wanting both Enrile and Ramos arrested for some reason. The latter two then called for an urgent press conference inside Camp Aguinaldo; they called for help and support from the people. At the same time, Cory Aquino launched a massive protest against Marcos on the result of fraudulent snap election; it was later on backed by religious and private sectors and the people power at EDSA. In a press conference, Enrile admitted two things: his participation in the conduct of electoral fraud in the 1986 snap elections against Cory Aquino and the staging of his September 1972 fake ambush at Wack-Wack Golf and Country Club the night before the Marcos's 1081 public proclamation of martial law.[68]

C. *Terrorism Turned into a Moneymaking Business*

This study reveals that some Islamic warlike extremists with potential leadership had seen the opportunities in forming rebel groups to gain national attention and international recognition with Al Qaeda linkage or Arab nations in the Middle East for financial support in a guise of Mindanao Muslim autonomy. Their modus operandi had been reported to have involved some military and police personnel conniving with terrorist bandits in facilitating kidnap-for-ransom business. The Philippine military said that Abu Sayyaf, an Al-Qaeda-linked Islamic group, was set up in 1990s with seed money from Osama Bin Laden, the leading international terrorist. It is possible that Raddulan Sahiron's claim may be true, that it was not so much on Mindanao issues that they are fighting for but the attractive seed money and support from Osama Bin Laden. In 1997, FBI put Raddulan Sahiron, the leader of the group, on US terror blacklist when he kidnapped and held an American citizen hostage for twenty-three days in Jolo Island. He was indicted in a US federal court in 2007 and believed to be responsible for the nation's worst terrorist attacks.[69]

The terrorist-linked group may commit criminal acts and instill fear in the community. It is their way of getting national and international recognition to gain financial support from the Arab nations. Eventually, it turned into a good business. According to a *Manila Times* news report, the Abu Sayyaf Group, an Al-Qaeda-linked terrorist, and other organized syndicate criminals have turned their kidnapping-for-ransom activities into a lucrative business according to the local officials in Southern Mindanao, Philippines. The organized criminals do the kidnappings and pass it on to Abu Sayyaf for a cut of the ransom money. The whereabouts of several kidnapped foreigners are unknown even until now. It is either they are still alive in the hands of their kidnappers or they are already cold and dead because the government and their home country do not want to deal with their kidnappers.[70]

On October 5, 2012, United States Undersecretary of the treasury David Cohen spoke at Chatham House about kidnapping for ransom as part of the terrorist financing method. The terrorists raised a significant amount from kidnapping for ransom in the early of 2012. In the past eight years, the terrorists had collected about $120 million from this sort of financing methods. Cohen pointed out that it is very disturbing what the terrorists can do with the money. Several millions of dollars were raised by Taliban in Pakistan, while the Abu Sayyaf Group in the Philippines acquired more than $2 million from ransom money. They used the ransom money to fund all their activities and operation. David Cohen, in his speech, discussed the new modus operandi of the terrorists. They turned to kidnapping for ransom to raise funds needed for their operations. They have discovered a significant source of income proven to be frightening tactics but effective and successful. It is now a great concern that if potential criminals will learn the methods and tactics of this trade, it might encourage future kidnappers to engage in this type of business.[71]

D. *Connivance - Military and Abu Sayyaf*

According to Philippine Ambassador Jim Lehrer, it is difficult to capture the Abu Sayyaf Group because the military needs advanced equipment, which they can conveniently use in the terrains of Basilan and Jolo, to go after them. However, after a thorough investigation of two journalists, Marites Vitug and Glenda Gloria, they found out that the possible reason the military and local police have failed to capture the terrorists is, according to reports that they receive, the cuts of the ransom monies from the bandit groups. It was confirmed by a Roman Catholic priest in a congressional hearing. He narrated what he once witnessed in a hospital compound where the ransom exchange was held. The military created a drama to allow the Abu Sayyaf kidnappers escape with their remaining hostages.

Author Madge Kho pointed out in her article, "Fighting the Abu Sayyaf: A Pretext for US Intervention in the Philippines," that the kidnapping events in the Philippines serve as a way of Gloria Arroyo's administration to get more monetary assistance from the United States for antiterrorism program although the Philippines had already received $4.2 billion antiterrorism foreign aid since the 9/11 event.[72]

Gracia Burnham, who was kidnapped from a resort in Palawan while she and her husband were celebrating their wedding anniversary, revealed the possible military involvement in the kidnap-for-ransom operation of the Abu Sayyaf. She described how they were taken by boat toward Cagayan de Sulu, then to Basilan Island. She said they sailed for several days before they reached the islands. She also revealed how they were treated by the kidnappers, the lost ransom money in the hands of the military or police, and the corrupt military involved in the negotiation of the price for ransom money with the kidnappers.[73] If the military were serious about intercepting them while on the ocean, they could have a helicopter follow them immediately and catch them. If none even one, how come a military helicopter, with military and government officials aboard, was always seen flying over the areas during devastating calamities or flood?

E. *Terrorism – Good Bait for Foreign Financial Aid*

Terrorism is a good bait for wealth and money. It could be one of the reasons why the war on terrorism or against Islamic fanaticism and fundamentalism continues. That's why this war on terror in the Philippines can never be won by high-powered weapons, bombings, and huge US military support. It may just lead to military corruption, continuous terroristic activities, and dependency.

In a similar situation, the US military aid to Afghanistan was under scrutiny in the US Senate. They wanted to find out how it's being used and evaluate the result of it. The report indicated that the $19 billion US aid to Afghanistan may have encouraged dependency of Afghanistan on the United States and corruption in the country. Both isles in the US Senate questioned and scrutinized the progress and the outcome of the ten-year US aid to stabilize Afghanistan. The Philippines and Afghanistan are both third-world countries, with similar insurgency or terrorism problem, and have been receiving US military aid for counterterrorism funds; but it seems both have same effects and terrorism never ends.[74]

The *New York Times* also reported that the US aid to the Philippines has done more advantages to the Islamic militants than the Philippine military because of corruption and malpractices in the Armed Forces of the Philippines (AFP). The Philippine military had not improved despite of continuous flow of US military aid. It would be more beneficial to the Philippine government if the United States were to amend its military aid to the Philippines and focus on providing literacy, proper education, and economic development to poor Muslims areas in Southern Philippines. Consequently, because of US new policies, the military budget might significantly decrease unless the Philippine government can guarantee the arms transfer to the Philippine military. It's a sad thing to note that US-branded weapons recovered at the enemies' camp may be used to fight or kill US military. The US government gave the Philippines $340 million in aid this year, but still, President Arroyo requested additional assistance for the AFP. Because of a widespread corruption in the military, three hundred young military officers were disgruntled, rebelled, and eventually tried to unseat the Pres. G. M. Arroyo because of their discontentment and belief that it's all directly or indirectly tolerated by Pres. Gloria M. Arroyo.[75]

F. *Politicians Corrupted the Law Enforcement System*

In another scenario, the police were unable to function effectively for lack of funds. I remember a mother of a fifteen-year-old girl came to me crying for help. She begged me to rescue her daughter on board a boat on the way to Manila from the hands of human traffickers. I took her to a police station and asked the chief of police to intercept them before the boat docked at the port of Manila.

The police gave a frustrating response, saying, "Sorry, sir, we don't have radio equipment."

I asked further to find ways by calling Camp Crame in Manila by cell phone, but he answered, "Who's going to pay for the phone call, sir, and who's going to pay for her fare in coming back?" That was very disgusting.

During the Marcos administration, I used to go to the office of the National Intelligence Security Agency (NISA) in our city to contact government and military agencies in times of crisis and emergency. They could right away call Camp Crame or direct to Malacañang Office in urgent situations. But in this case, with latest communication technology, I was frustrated because there was nothing they can do to rescue the girl.

Another instance, when I made a complaint to the police station to subpoena someone for criminal action against damages done to personal properties, the police said, "We need to fill up gas, sir, for the motorcycle to deliver the subpoena."

They said the police don't have enough funds to do their job. One of our neighbors was a victim of holdup, robbery, and car napping. They immediately called the police after the culprits left with their brand new

"Toyota Pick Up." Unfortunately, the police only came to investigate the next day. They could have intercepted the vehicle before it could get out of the area because there were only two ways out from the area.

After all these, I had a chance to talk to the newly assigned chief of police. I asked him why they could not properly respond to citizens' crises. In a low tone of voice, he told me that it's because of lack of funds in the police department. This information confirmed what I heard from the news about some issues of a certain local government official who diverted the allotted police "intelligence fund". A faithful Christian police chief, newly assigned in a certain city, tendered his request for reassignment right away, even before he assumed office. He was presented by a government official with intelligence fund voucher for his signature that he received the funds. He refused to sign and tendered his request for transfer right away. These are all verbal information but confirm why the police personnel are demoralized and powerless.

As members of a gun club, we decided to invite members of the police department to join a shooting competition. To our surprise, they refused for lack of supply of bullets. One police officer said, "If I join and use my supply of ten bullets, nothing would be left." Poor police officer!

In preparation for APEC Summit 2015 in the Philippines, I conducted a lecture on how to secure the APEC Summit and how to investigate cases involving foreign dignitaries during the CIDG regional conference. During lunchtime, three provincial chief investigators, with their regional chief intelligence officers, engaged me in a friendly conversation. They confessed of planning to retire from their job soon. They told me that they didn't want to wait to have charges filed by politicians against them. They cited a case they filed against a certain individual for the alleged illegal possession of firearms and explosives. To their frustration, a certain government official called their attention why they messed with his men. They heard later that the confiscated weapons used as evidence were returned to the suspect upon presentation of a doubtful or backdated document. I could see low morale and frustration in their faces.

How could the law enforcers accomplish their jobs if someone's voice from the higher up seems to be higher than the law?

When corrupt politicians and government officials interfere and impose what they want into the law enforcement system, it cripples and makes the law enforcers powerless and hesitant in doing their jobs for fear of getting fired, transferred, or face countercharges initiated by someone higher in the government filed against them.

Pres. George W. Bush of the United States kept reiterating that the best defense is offense, which means the United States should run after the terrorists and hunt them abroad and into the lands before they can reach the United States. As part of an offensive strategy, he gave antiterrorism funds and promised more US military aid to Pres. Gloria M. Arroyo, who was representing the first nation to declare support and accept the challenge to fight terrorism; she was probably the first president to visit the White House after the September 11, 2001 incident. The report showed that the United States, in the late 1980s, extended assistance to the Philippine armed forces and law enforcers in trying to improve their ability to combat the communist insurgents.

In the years 1986–1989, the United States sent 2,900 military vehicles, about 50 helicopters, more than 1,650 radios, 225 military uniforms, including more than 150,000 pairs of combat shoes, and assorted infantry weapons, ammunition, and medical equipment. After all those assistance and increased budgets and growing foreign military aid, the Philippine Armed Forces is still considered the most poorly funded and less equipped military in Asia. The study concluded that the Armed Forces of the Philippines had endured limited resources, such as shortages of military vehicles, helicopters, radios, spare parts, medicines, and clothing. It was because of the inefficient logistics system, red tape, corruption, and poor living and working condition of the military, which became the underlying cause of military disciple problems. In the 1990s, top military officials had seen these problems and tried to correct this deficiency, but their so-called modernizing the military had received little funding and many WWII nave ships were increasingly very difficult to maintain. The Philippine Air Force was also undergoing similar issues, and the modernization of the military is still a dream.[76] Larry Nischk revealed that from January up to July 2002 alone, the Philippines received another $93 million to fight the Abu Sayyaf, but despite of US military financial assistance, the struggle continued and Abu Sayyaf engaged in recruitment, training, and kidnap-for-ransom operations. These dramatic kidnap-for-ransom activities became more internationally popular and may have turned into a good business and fund-raising to support terroristic activities.[77]

MR. ANO WHO

G. *The Corruption Inside the Military*

1. *The FSGO Official Response to Gen. Angelo Reyes's Suicide*

The Former Senior Government Officials (FSGO), a group of former members of the cabinet, released a statement in response to the recent controversy of the suicide of Gen. Angelo Reyes. A portion of their statement said,

> *"The death of Gen. Reyes reminds us that corruption kills. Most often, it kills poor Filipinos with hunger, disease, disaster or crime because the money meant to help or protect them was stolen. It kills soldiers whose bullets ran out, whose guns fail, whose trucks ran out of gasoline, whose aircraft crashed due to poor maintenance, all because someone stole the money for their needs. Sometimes, corruption kills those that partake of its evil fruit."[78]*

The entire statement emphasized that almost no one in the Senate and government agencies gave any attention nor made any serious attempt to expose the corruption happening within them, not even the legal and criminal agencies. They stated further that the death of Angelo Reyes reminded everyone that corruption can cost life and most of the time the victims are the poor Filipinos suffering from hunger, disease, disaster, or crime because the money that was supposedly to provide for their needs was stolen by undeserving government official. They also emphasized that even the regular soldiers were affected because the money intended to advance their equipment was gone. It is probably not only true in the Philippines but even in other agencies and governments in the entire globe also.

In an article on corruption, Anup Shah stated,

> *"Corruption is both a major cause and a result of poverty around the world. It occurs at all levels of society, from local and national governments, civil society, judiciary functions, large and small businesses, military and other services and so on . . . Corruption affects the poorest the most, in rich or poor nations, though all elements of society are affected in some way*

as corruption undermines political development, democracy, economic development, the environment, people's health and more."[79]

Only a callous and greedy heart could never understand or feel the effects of corruption when people are dying of hunger, malnutrition, and sickness for lack of food, medicines, and health treatments just because funds were stolen by someone in the government. When I visited a friend who was admitted in a public hospital, I saw an overflowing number of patients waiting in line for treatment. Most of them were very poor and couldn't afford to buy medicines. They were waiting in line for their turn only to receive a piece of paper (written prescription) from their attending physician, while some of the patients were dying in agony of pain. Sometimes patients are ignored for lack of financial capacity to pay hospital services. The national and local governments have annual budget for medical supplies and medicines but probably not enough to meet the needs of most needy ones when funds are diverted and drained to the government officials and employees' pockets. Some of the patients either died without seeing a doctor or before treatment. I have a friend who used to be a supply officer at a nationally funded provincial hospital who always jokingly talked about suppliers and dealers doing business through her office. She narrated how the monkey business system goes on in the provincial hospital management. She told me some serious questions of the patients. A patient asked the doctor who gave him some sample medicines given by medical representatives or suppliers. The patient said, "Doctor, are there any side effects in this medicine?"

The doctor responded, "Wala ngang effect, side effect pa ba?" (If there is no effect, how can it have side effects?)

The reduced or lowered the quality of locally made drugs that are usually delivered by suppliers for price adjustment and the so-called Standard Operating Procedure (SOP) requirement. That means no transaction made without under the table deal at the expense of good and effective medicines. The SOP goes to people involved in the process. She narrated that in doing business with government hospitals; both the provincial health officer (PHO) and the assigned Commission On Audit (COA) officer would not sign the vouchers or purchase orders without "under the table" commitment from the dealers. In this case, huge amounts of money for overpriced supplies are being corrupted at the expense of good health services for the less fortunate constituents. Their callous and insensitive hearts and conscience are already numb, watching the suffering and dying untreated patients in line daily because of lack of medicines. Every year their approved budget for medical supplies and medicines based on the needs and numbers of patients could have possibly been drained into the pockets of some government officials and employees. I suspect that he same is true to some government agencies, and it could also happen in the military institution. There are retired rich military generals or military officials who could already afford to join politics on a national level. Maybe some are still active, brave, and courageous enough to see uniformed men and civilian victims die in terroristic drama or sabotage for money?

2. *The Corruption of UN Military Assistance*

It is now exposed that aside from the US military financial assistance, the Philippines also received funding from the United Nations. When the Philippine senators questioned the incumbent and former COA officials during a Senate hearing, they uncovered some irregularities in the Armed Forces of the Philippines modernization fund. They uncovered over a billion pesos of UN fund remittances given to the AFP from 2001 to 2004. They also questioned the use of intermediary banks in General Santos City and Iloilo City in the AFP's transactions and why the funds from the United Nations were not used as intended.[80]

3. *Pres. Benigno C. Aquino III Confirmed There Is Corruption in the Military*

Corruption is not unknown to the highest office in the government, the office of the president. When Pres. Benigno C. Aquino III attended the annual alumni homecoming of the Philippine Military Academy (PMA) in Baguio City, he spoke in connection with his campaign against corruption, not only among the military personnel but also the corrupt Supreme Court justices in the country, the first in Philippine history. He expressed his full support for the investigation of corruption in the Armed Forces of the Philippines (AFP). He suspected that there were high-ranking government officials involved and behind those people accused of corruption.[81]

This misuse of funds may not only be true in the Philippines, but even in countries recipient of U.S. Military Aid that the United States might have overlooked in a similar situation. There are also high-ranking government officials in other countries that enriched themselves at the expense of good governance and national security. In Pakistan, corruption is not a secret. They have been receiving US military aid to fight terrorism and extremist enemies. Providing changes in government oversight system may effectively prevent corruption using a dedicated monitoring group that understands how and when the US aid should be used. The same should have been done in the Philippines, not only to prevent terrorism but also corruption in the military; government officials continue fighting, and the misuse of US military funds should be a US government concern. According to the information, the Pakistani military counterterrorism efforts failed because of misuse of funds, and the United States may have been improperly handling its funds against terror and might have been using American tax payers' money to fund corruption in Pakistan too.[82] The United States has been giving funds to Pakistan for counterterrorism, assuming that they will use it as intended. The Coalition Support Fund is supposed to reimburse Pakistan military expenditures limited to fighting terrorism only, assuming that the weapons of $9.7 billion worth from 2002 to 2007 will be used for counterterrorism and the Pakistani government expects the United States to reimburse it. Large portion of the US military aid was used to purchase military equipment instead of fighting terrorism as intended, resulting to "billing disputes" over the US military funds and more than 40 percent of unsubstantiated or exaggerated claims have been rejected by the US government.[83]

4. *Former Navy Officer/Senator Confirmed Military Corruption*

Another scenario revealed that the US counterterrorism assistance fund enticed corruption. A former Philippine Navy officer who led a military mutiny and currently a member of the Senate, LTJG Antonio F. Trillanes, in his interviews with media, stated that there's a big possibility that Pres. Gloria M. Arroyo, who is currently in prison for corruption charges, was involved in the military corruption, wherein millions of pesos and huge amount of money from the military funds were stolen during her administration.[84] While taking his master's degree at the University of the Philippines, LTJG Antonio F. Trillanes, now member of the Senate, previously conducted a research on corruption, particularly in the military. In his thesis, he cited some specific issues and incidents of corruption involving military officials with Pres. Gloria Arroyo's knowledge and tolerance at the expense of the country's development and national security. The Philippine Navy's mission was derailed because of corruption and even cost many innocent lives. Trillanes was one of three hundred junior rebel officers and enlisted men who took over the Oakwood Premier in the Ayala Center and protested against the alleged corruption in the military and demanded the resignation of Pres. Gloria Arroyo and other officials in the military. In his conclusion, he further said that corruption problem in the navy is grave and caused direct and indirect devastating damages to our economy and national security.[85]

5. *Two Retired Government Budget Officers Confirmed Military Corruption*

Another witness, a retired budget officer, Perla Valero, testified before the Senate Hearing Committee against the alleged corruption in the military. She facilitated diversion of funds from officials' discretionary funds for unofficial purposes with the instruction and approval of her bosses. It confirms the earlier testimony of the previous witness that cash was given to top military officials.[86]

One more witness, George Rabusa, a former budget officer, said that Cong. Prospero Pichay, Jr., was a recipient of diverted military funds. Rabusa also said that Maj. Gen. Carlos Garcia instructed him to give P500,000 to Pichay at least three times. He prepared the money for Pichay every time he visited the office of Diomedio Villanueva, chief of staff of the Armed Forces of the Philippines (AFP).

At that time, Pichay was the chairman of the House Committee on National Defense.[87]

With all the above credible military officials and other government employees' revelation of the rampant corruption of military funds, these maybe enough to prove that the US military aid makes beneficiary governments or military officials corrupt, which is caused by not only greed but also the continuous flow of enticing millions of foreign financial assistance to countries, such as the Philippines.

6. *The US Military Aid Prolonged the War against Terror*

Despite of the alleged lack of resources, Pres. Gloria Arroyo was still personally convinced that the Philippine military had enough strength to topple down terrorists. It's possible that she already anticipated the true strength of the Abu Sayyaf Group, and when the US military Special Forces arrived for the Balikatan Exercise in Jolo, Sulu, they could certainly discover how powerless and small the Abu Sayyaf Group that could escape in small islands that the military could never capture them.

Then as the commander in chief of the armed forces, she ordered the military to wipe out the extremist Abu Sayyaf in ninety days when the United States positioned to send military advisers in the following month to Sulu under the US-Philippine Balikatan training program and joint military exercise in the use of modern infantry weapons in Southern Mindanao. Before the US military forces arrived, she issued a directive amid kidnappings for ransom, which the military armed forces have failed to neutralize terrorist activities and reinstate normalcy in the region despite of foreign military assistance. When I saw the islands in Sulu, I wondered why the AFP or the law enforcers could not catch the bandits. If the military could not protect the people in a very small island, how could they provide safety to the entire country? The bandits are not equipped with powerful speedboats. Why are the kidnappers' untouchables? Pres. Gloria Arroyo was convinced that the Philippine military had enough resources to extinguish extremist groups in such short span of time, even without US assistance. Just before Arroyo went to the White House to meet President Bush, Arroyo ordered the military to finish the Abu Sayyaf. Arroyo said,

"I've given the Military a deadline to finish the Abu Sayyaf in 90 days . . . I suppose the military will be able to meet the deadline if they properly allocate their resources. They'll be able to finish the Abu Sayyaf in 90 days . . ."[88]

The ninety days had passed; Abu Sayyaf's terroristic activities still continued.

In this juncture, it seems that the US military counterterrorism assistance to the Philippines may have prolonged the fight rather than end it.

In a very small island, the Abu Sayyaf could have been wiped out in a very short span of time, considering their numbers, but when Pres. Gloria M. Arroyo met Pres. G. W. Bush at the White House, as the first country to support the idea of attacking Iraq, she received millions of dollars for antiterrorism assistance, and in the succeeding years, she received more antiterrorism campaign fund from the United States, but the fight still goes on. Evidently, the US military aid for counterterrorism may have caused more corruption and more drama of terrorism.

CHAPTER 8

The Philippines For More Military Aid.

A COMMENTARY ON MILITARY assistance to the Philippines states that the Philippines and the United States have a mutual defense treaty in effect since 1952, and the total US military assistance to the Philippines up to the year 2005 alone was projected at US$164 million. The Philippines is the fourth largest recipient of US foreign military aids, also of Australia, as reportedly the major source of military assistance.[89] Another source of information stated that in 2009, the total Australian aid contribution to the Philippines totaled to AU$ 123 million. A proportion of this sum went to the AFP. After the United States, Australia was the second largest supplier of military aid to the Philippines. There were about 130 AFP officers brought to Australia each year for training in intelligence gathering and other dubious activities.[90]

The above information evidently showed that an antiterrorism program is a good bait to draw more foreign financial aid for both the terrorist group and the government. It could serve as a source of power and wealth for those who are leading the government and those who are suspiciously behind the terroristic drama.

At this stage, with the huge sum of foreign financial aid for antiterrorism from the USA and other nations, the Philippines could have recruited more military personnel, schools, and educators. With an economic aid program, the most neglected region of the country could have been seriously developed. But if the military and government officials continue the exploitation of terrorism for political interest and turn national security or peace and order issue into a business, in a guise of the antiterrorism program, then terrorism in the country would never end.

During a news conference in Manila on April 11, 2012, with Albert Del Rosario, the Philippine foreign affairs secretary, he told the reporters that the United States would triple its military aid to the Philippines.[91] Let's just hope for the best that there is already some restrictive measure that would prevent misuse or corruption of funds in the hands of the current and succeeding administrations.

In another report, the Philippines would seek more military equipment and training assistance to counter China's intrusion on the disputed islands in South China Sea. Gen. Gregorio Catapang drafted a "wish list" for the Philippine foreign affairs secretary Albert Del Rosario's trip to the United States to ask for more US aid to develop Philippine armed forces' capabilities, focusing on maritime security. Hundreds of Filipinos and US marines would be trained in an amphibious assault to reclaim territory from invaders.[92]

What could the Philippine government give as guarantee to avoid this culture of corruption in the government or military? While traveling throughout the country, I have personally witnessed police officers and military agents selling brand new weapons made in the USA despite of their claim that they lack good or sophisticated weapons, equipment, and ammunition. What happened to U.S Military supplies intended the Armed Forces of the Philippines? On one occasion, a military intelligence officer I met tried to sell me a brand new US-made .45 pistol. I knew it was illegal, as it was still in a sealed envelope. Where did these weapons come from? Its package was still in sealed plastics.

CHAPTER 9

US Military Weapons and Supplies Landed in the Wrong Hands?

THE REPORT REVEALED that at least fifty-four refurbished M16 rifles intended for the provincial police were sold to local politicians. Some of the guns illegally held and kept for personal use by retired cops; other guns were sold. These are just some of the anomalies involving government-issued weapons uncovered in Autonomous Region in Muslim Mindanao (ARMM). The *Philippine Star* reported that the Ampatuan clan had built up an enormous private army and had free access to PNP vehicles, equipment, and weaponry.[93]

The reports further said that at least 10 percent of the seized weapons appeared to have been sourced from the military, while the rest are from private arms dealers. The report went on that the Ampatuans have enough stock of weapons and thousands of ammunitions and ten armored vehicles enough to supply two army battalions. Aside from weapons, the military also recovered 430,000 ammunitions (including bullets). Huge supplies of ammunition in boxes still have markings of Philippine National Police and the government arsenal of the Department of National Defense.[94]

Another reporter alleged that after the massacre in Maguindanao on November 23, 2009, that killed at least fifty-seven people, an investigation was conducted, including the surroundings of the Ampatuan clan's residences. The investigators uncovered ammunitions and assorted weapons of 274 licensed firearms, excluding the unlicensed.

Two months later, they uncovered another assorted 1,200 firearms around the residence of the Amapatuans, the political kingpin of one of the country's poorest provinces, now a suspect in the gruesome killing of journalists and political rivals on their way to filing a certificate of candidacy. The investigation reports concerning the Ampatuans' weapons traced back to the government as the source of these firearms, and there were still more undiscovered high-tech arms with higher caliber. Some of them were identified coming from the AFP arsenal and PNP armory; there were marks of AFP and PNP on it. The report further said that there were still thirty to forty thousand or more loose firearms in ARMM provinces.[95] These weapons could never be released to the political kingpin Ampatuan family in Cotabato and individuals without high-ranking officials in the government and military involved. In 2014, the Philippine military spending was $2.6 billion, just a dot compared to China's $132 billion annual military budget. But the Philippine government focused its resources on improving its monitoring capabilities and responding to South China Sea developments. The US assistance contributed so much to Philippine efforts against terrorism, but why does the Philippine military still lack modern capabilities, including intelligence platforms, adequate logistical support, and reliable casualty evacuation capability? The total US military assistance to the Philippines rose from US$38 million in 2001 to US$114 million in 2003 to a projected US$164 million in 2005, thus making the Philippines the fourth largest US foreign military assistance recipient; other countries like Australia were also reported to be a major source of military aid.[96]

CHAPTER 10

Recommendation

A. *Implement GAO's Recommendation*

ACCORDING TO US Government Audit Office (GAO) analysis of the national security assistance strategy, the United States has no coherent and clear strategic policy that satisfied the US Congress's expectation, and it only deprived the necessary information needed for decision-makings in the future. There was no collective national assistance strategy that has addressed some objectives for legislative measure. GAO recommended that the secretary of state should address the following:

1. *Establish stronger management controls evaluating security forces abroad by clearly defining existing guidelines.*
2. *Prepare a periodic report to Congress an integrated strategic plan for all U.S. government assistance that provides training and equipment for security forces abroad.*[97]

Following GAO's recommendation, it is then necessary for the US government to impose external rules that would manage the flow of funds from the United States, not only to the Philippines, rules that can extensively and accurately audit and appropriately allocate funds to ensure it would be used for the good of many, not for the sake of one man and military generals in power. So the American tax payer's money would not be misused or wasted.

B. *More on Education and Economic Development*

Based on information gathered in this research, it is recommended or suggested that America should provide more assistance to education and economic development with accountability because education is a good tool for changing the hearts and minds of the people. Education changes a person's behavior and perspective in life. Economic development is proven to be more effective in winning the hearts and allegiance of the less fortunate people, particularly the poor Muslim community, in which literacy and economic depression are the utmost concerns, for they are the most vulnerable people to terroristic ideology. The same is true in the non-Muslim community, where the New People's Army (NPA) is very effective in their propaganda using the issues on corruption, military abuses, and economic depression. That's why most of those who participated in terrorism come from Muslim constituents. They are the ones who suffer the scarcity of educational materials and lack of quality education. The idea presented that those who experience societal injustice become aggressive to activism. Addressing the real issues and grievances through proper education, their societal anger will turn to moral anger. Talia Miriam Master indicated in her thesis also that it is possible for a person to transform their anger into moral anger and subsequently into activism. Individuals who experience moral anger often perceive their anger as righteous and justified, linked to something greater than individual self-interest.

Taking the opinion of Talia Master, we can assume that quality education can change the way people believe, and instead of tolerating societal anger driven by hatred and revenge, people can transform their moral anger into something that would desire unity and peace.[98]

While there are many less educated Muslims who turned themselves criminals and warlike people, there are also many professional and educated Muslims who act respectful and righteous like anybody else who would condemn extremism; they make a living peacefully because of proper education. Nabil Tan's experience is a good an example. He was born in 1959 in Sulu and raised as a Muslim. He became deputy governor of Autonomous Region in Muslim Mindanao (ARMM) for seventeen years, engaging in the peace process with the Moro Islamic Liberation Front (MILF). Nabil Tan expressed his feelings being educated in a Roman Catholic school which he learned to respect all religious beliefs despite of being raised as a Muslim. He said that he was grateful to receive a Catholic education, for it helped him respect the differences of faith and encouraged him to engage in dialogue for peace in Mindanao. Nabil Tan attended Notre Dame Catholic School from kindergarten to high school and graduated with a degree in law from the Philippine Muslim College. Affirming the good result of education, he further shared that the education and values he received since childhood influenced his whole life. He let them rule his life, and it led him to a righteous life with a passion for serving his countrymen, especially those who are in need. In their school, they were taught to respect different faiths. Their American teacher would let each one of them recite morning prayers according to their faith. Nabil Tan also has been participating and celebrating Christmas, exchanging gifts as well; he also celebrates Ramadan with Christians in the community.[99] While it's a proven fact that education changes a person's perspectives in life and could be a good weapon to win the hearts and minds of the people, America seems to spend more dollars in bombs and weapons to win the war rather than infiltrate through education and economic assistance to poor countries infested with terrorism.

C. *Familiarity with "Quraysh Model" - Mohammed's Revolutionary Principle*

In dealing with Islamic extremist or terrorist groups, the AFP or governments must be aware of Mohammed's Quraysh model strategy applied by these revolutionaries. The Islamic warlike people have inherited the Quraysh model principle from their Prophet Mohammed who used it during his revolutionary life. In times of war, he said, "Negotiate peace with your enemy until you become strong enough to annihilate him." This principle was used by Chairman Yasser Arafat to justify his signing of the Oslo Agreement when condemned by his critics.[100]

The government must be very careful in negotiating with the Islamic extremists groups or terrorists. There were different instances that the Philippine government attempted to make peace with the Islamic groups, but the treaty had been violated, and the fight continued. One instance when a ceasefire was decided and declared by both sides, they decided to meet for a common ground.

Brig. Gen. Teodulfo Bautista and his troops, without arms or weapons, were on their way to Jolo, Sulu, for peace-talk agreement with MNLF when they got ambushed by armed Muslim groups. The soft-spoken Brig. Gen. Teodulfo Bautista, the commanding general of the First Infantry "Tabak" Division of the Philippine Army, and his thirty-four men were brutally massacred and defenselessly died. They were lured or trapped into a peaceful dialogue by Usman Sali, a rebel leader in Patikul, Sulu.[101]

When dealing with Islamic groups, the Philippine government and the armed forces should familiarize the revolutionary tactics of Mohammed during his revolutionary life. They should seriously learn the Islamic tradition of these Al-Qaeda-linked groups to avoid risky negotiations and get rid of corrupt military and government officials. The greed of money had already lost thousands of innocent lives. The kidnap-for-ransom business, rebellion, and terrorism at the expense of economy and peace and order have to stop. The Filipinos must be aware and vigilant of any artificially or politically motivated chaos and turmoil to gain power in government. May the pieces of evidence presented in this research provide significant and useful information to the concerned citizens of the republic.

To all members of the New People's Army (NPA) and other Al Qaeda-linked group members, you know that thousands of your members are living in hunger and some had already died while the founding leaders are partying and having a luxurious lifestyle in a beautiful country. Whether politically motivated or created by someone out of greed of money and power, only their conscience could tell and confirm. Please don't let them exploit you and let's stop killing one another while the founding leaders are gaining wealth and power because of the attractive millions of foreign assistance.

All these recommendations above come down to one claim: In order to stop terrorism and to prevent the loss of more lives, it would be best for the US government to focus more on education and economic development, for we could not win this war with bombs and weapons. Education is the best weapon to combat terroristic ideologies with economic development to provide economic stability to poor communities in the country. Without corruption, the amount of US financial assistance to the Philippines could have hired well-trained educators and recruited thousands of military personnel and police officers nationwide to prevent and fight terrorism in our country. Oftentimes we hear reports from the media that the Philippine government lacks military and police personnel, vehicles, weapons, ammunitions, and communication equipment to respond to criminalities. These are the common reasons of continuous unsolved cases and unaccomplished mission despite of millions of dollars of foreign assistance to the Philippines.

CHAPTER 11

Conclusion

THIS BOOK CONCLUDES that the long history of abuse and maltreatment experienced by the Filipino people from their oppressors played a major role in the development of their rebellious or terroristic attitude and behavior. As a result of the many years of struggle of the early Filipinos, an aggressive anti-colonialism spirit made them so untrusting to those who are in power and made them vulnerable to different ideologies, including the terroristic ones. In the long run, the Filipinos transformed from being hospitable natives into being an oppressed people, then became the struggling propagandist, determined resistant, and now aggressive terrorists against their own people. With all the above rationale, the United States should make a brilliant strategic policy in providing military aid to foreign countries, for it might just spoil the beneficiaries or encourage corruption that fuels terrorism, rather than preventing them.

Al-Qaeda is weakening and to call for all-out war against them must continue with new strategic methodology. Internationally, the Al-Qaeda's popularity and support are substantially slowing down after the death of Osama Bin Laden, but governments must continue to regard it as a threat to national security. Terrorism only flourished when the governments paid lesser concerns and considered it as infrequent activities. After the 9/11 incident, governments around the world prompted to engage in the war against terrorism in collaboration with the United States. The unity and effort of the countries worldwide in stopping terrorism also stopped the money that flows into the Al-Qaeda system.[102] Even before or after Osama Bin Laden's alleged death, Abu Sayyaf or the Al-Qaeda has been weakening because of diminishing flow of funds. In some areas in Mindanao, the MILF recruitments of new members became frustrating for those who joined because of unfulfilled promises to support the families that they left, and their cooperation with the rebels turned out nothing at all, and they returned to their families with an empty basket. The problem happened because Osama Bin Laden's financial empire had already collapsed, and he was already broke that he could no longer feed his followers. Terrorism in the Philippines could have died a natural death already for lack of financial support. Before Bin Laden's death, his group and his men were already demoralized and were having difficulties in their operation.[103]

If the US Department of Homeland Security would continue their intensified efforts in identifying and tracking down their sources of funds and the flow of international financial support for Al-Qaeda-linked groups, surely it will paralyze their operations. Without financial support, no one would be interested and attempt to join them.

With all these facts, we can assume that the United States is like fanning a dying fire of war when they gave out more funds to the Philippine military without accountability measure. Instead of ending the war, it had cost more lives of innocent victims.

The islands of Sulu, a haven for Al-Qaeda or terrorists, are very small; it's a wonder why the Philippine military cannot capture them. Therefore, it makes sense to believe that if the Philippine military continues to receive huge amounts of US financial assistance without accountability and the Abu Sayyaf, on the other side, also receives more funding from their foreign supporters; the drama of terrorism and kidnappings for ransom will go on. The creation of a superficial atmosphere of conflicts, chaos, and terroristic activities is possible. The prolonged war or fighting is a way to justify the consumption of funds and continues the need for more funds for counterinsurgency operation. Terrorism in the Philippines might have ended already, or it could have been easy to control if the US military aid to the Philippines properly addresses the real need of the neglected ones. If the fight and doubtful kidnap-for-ransom business continue, this will make the Philippines still qualified to receive a more additional substantial amount for antiterrorism campaign as part of the US foreign military aid program.[104]

REFERENCES

1. Merriam-Webster. (2015) An Encyclopedia Britannica Company: Rebellion. Retrieved: August 27, 2015. http://www.merriam-webster.com/dictionary/rebellion.

2. The Difference-Between Website, (n.d.) Home: Insurgency vs. Insurrection – What's the Difference: Retrieved: September 8, 2015. http://the-difference-between.com/insurrection/insurgency.

3. Department of Defense Dictionary of Military Terms (November 8, 2010 as amended through June 15, 2015).Terrorism. Retrieved: August 27, 2015. http://www.dtic.mil/doctrine/dod_dictionary/?zoom_query=+Terrorism&zoom_sort= 0&zoom_per_page=10&zoom_and=1.

4. Truth, Honesty and Justice Website. (July 14, 2002) The Alternative to Wars, Terrorism and Politics: Definition to Terrorism. Retrieved: August 27, 2025. http://www.truth-and-justice.info/defterror.html.

5. Wright, L. (2007, 279-280) The Looming Tower. Al Qaeda and the Road to 9/11. First Vintage Books Edition September 2007. www.vintagebooks.com.

6. Schiller, M. (2004) TvNewsLies.Org: Why George W. Bush Is the World's Leading Terrorist. Retrieved: January 9, 2013. http://www.tvnewslies.org/html/george_w__bush_-_world_s_leadi.html.

7. The FBI Albuquerque Division. (2012) What We Investigate? Retrieved: January 29, 2013. http://www.fbi.gov/albuquerque/about-us/what-we-investigate.

8. Schiller, M. (2004) TvNewsLies.Org: Why George W. Bush Is the World's Leading Terrorist. Retrieved: January 9, 2013. http://www.tvnewslies.org/html/george_w__bush_-_world_s_leadi.html.

9. Firdaus, I. (2006) Indonesian Protesters Tell Bush: You Are the terrorist. Retrieved: January 9, 2013. http://www.prisonplanet.com/articles/november2006/211106protesters.htm.

10. History.Com Website (August 2, 1990) This Day in History: Iraq Invades Kuwait. Retrieved: December 14, 2012. http://www. history.com/this-day-in-history/iraq-invades-kuwait.

11. Hussain, J. (August 4, 2012) Collateral Damage: The Rationale Behind the Invasion of Afghanistan Is Not Control of Oil and Gas. Retrieved: December 20, 2012. http://collateraldamagemagazine. com/2012   /08/04/the-rationale-behind-the-invasion-of-afghanistan-is-not-control-of-oil-and-gas/.

12. Gleason, K.C. (2005) Institute for Historical Review: The "Holocaust" and the Failure of Allied and Jewish Responses: The Logic of Disbelief. Retrieved: January 29, 2013. http://www.ihr. org/jhr/v05/v05p215_Gleason.html.

13. Glazer, S. D. (1914) My Jewish Learning. America and the Holocaust: Where Were the United States Government and the American Jewish Community During the Destruction of European Jewry? Retrieved: February 1, 2013. http://www. myjewishlearning.com/history/Modern_History/1914-

14. CBS News.com Website (March 6, 2013). Much of $60B from U.S. to Rebuild Iraq Wasted Special Auditor's Final Report to Congress Shows. Retrieved: August 28, 2015. http://www. cbsnews.com/news/much-of-60b-from-us-to-rebuild-iraq-wasted-special-auditors-final-report-to-congress-shows/.

15. Agoncillo, T. A. (1990, p. 71) History of the Filipino People. Garo Tech Books Inc., Quezon City Agoncillo, T. A. (1990, p. 71) History of the Filipino People. Eight Edition. Reprinted in (2012), C&E Publishing, Inc., 839 EDSA, South Triangle, Quezon City, Philippines.

16. Dejarme, E. G. (2006, pp. 215–226) Philippine History and Government: Growth of Nationalism St. Augustine Publications, Inc., Manila Philippines. www.staugustine publications.com.ph.

17. Ibid., 2006, pp. 216–220.

18. Flanagan, P. and Schihl, R. (2004) Catholic Biblical Apologetics, © Copyright 1985–2004. Retrieved: April 2, 2016. http://www. catholicapologetics.org/ap070400.htm.

19. Agoncillo, T. A. (1990, pp. 45–47). History of the Filipino People. Eight Edition. Reprinted in (2012), C&E Publishing, Inc., 839 EDSA, South Triangle, Quezon City, Philippines.

20. Ibid., 1990, p. 50.

21. Holy Bible (Acts 10:26, NKJV).

22. Holy Bible (Acts 14:13–15, NJKV).

23. Holy Bible (Revelation 19:10; 22:8–9, NJKV).

24. Religion in Ancient Rome. (n.d.) Retrieved: August 15, 2015. http://www.crystalinks.com/romereligion.html.

25. Dejarme, E. G. (2006, p. 137) Philippine History and Government: Growth of Nationalism St. Augustine Publications, Inc., Manila Philippines. www.staugustine publications.com.ph.

26. New World Encyclopedia (January 1, 2006) Douglas Mac Arthur: Japanese Invasion. Retrieved: January 3, 2013. http://www.newworldencyclopedia.org/entry/Douglas_MacArthur.

27. Eber, M. (n. d.) Profiling Osama. Retrieved: January 6, 2013. http://www.nyu.edu/classes/keefer/joe/eber1.html.

28. Neuman, J. (May 27, 2012) Danilel Pipes: Middle East Forum. Retrieved: July 25, 2015. http://www.danielpipes.org/comments/195861#comment_submit.

29. Philippine History (February 12, 2014) Philippine Independence from the Americans. Retrieved: October 22, 2015. http://www.philippine-history.org/independence-from-americans.htm.

30. The History Guy: The Philippine-American War 1899–1902. Retrieved August 12, 2015. http://www.historyguy.com/PhilipineAmericanwar.html#.Vcz9Z7JVikr.

31. Dumindin, A. (n.d.) Philippine-American War 1899–1902. Retrieved: August 25, 2015. http://philippineamericanwar.webs.com/filamwarbreaksout.htm.

32. YouTube (November 17, 2012) American Genocide in the Philippines /Filipines. https : //w w w.youtube.com/watch?v=dLWFF9ycmQs.

33. The Philippine History Website. (n.d.) The Philippine-American War: Introduction; American Campaign of Brutality; The Balangiga Massacre. Retrieved: January 7, 2013. http://opmanong.ssc.hawaii.edu/filipino/philam.html.

34. Philippine History Site. (n.d.) Philippine-American War: American Campaign of Brutality. Retrieved: September 23, 2015. http://opmanong.ssc.hawaii.edu/filipino/brutality.html.

35. The Japanese Occupation of the Philippines. Retrieved: J u l y 2 0 , 2 015 . ht t p s : / / e n .w i k i pe d ia . o rg / w i k i / Japanese_occupation_of_the_Philippines.

36. Dejarme, E. G. (2006, p. 311) Philippine History and Government: Growth of Nationalism St. Augustine Publications, Inc., Manila Philippines. www.staugustine publications.com.ph.

37. Campaign for Nuclear Disarmament. The Bombing of Hiroshima and Nagasaki. Retrieved: May 4, 2016. http://www.cnduk.org/campaigns/global-abolition/hiroshima-a-nagasaki.

38. Encyclopedia Britannica. Manuel Roxas-President of the Philippines. Retrieved: May 4, 2016. *http://www.britannica.com/biography/Manuel-Roxas-y-Acuna*.

39. Agoncillo, T. A. (2012, pp.110–111). History of the Filipino People. C & E Publishing, Inc. Eight Edition.

40. Dejarme, E. G. (2006, pp. 188–197). Philippine History and Government: Growth of Nationalism St. Augustine Publications, Inc., Manila Philippines. www.staugustine publications.com.ph.

41. Ibid., pp. 198–199.

42. Ibid., pp. 216–217.

43. Ibid., pp. 233–226.

44. The Philippine Consulate General Website (2012) About the Philippines: History. Level 1, Philippine Center 27-33 Wentworth Ave., Sydney NSW 2000. Retrieved: December 25, 2012. http://www.philippineconsulate.com.au/component/content/article/19-general-information/101-about-the-philippines.html.

45. Master, T. M. (2009) The Link Between Moral Anger and Social Activism: An Exploratory Study. New Brunswick, New Jersey.

46. Elloso, R. O.(2012, p. 8) *Philippine Panorama*. Sunday Magazine of *Manila Bulletin*, November 25 issue: Andres Bonifacio-Writer and Hero. *Manila Bulletin*, Newspaper Publication, Manila, Philippines.

47. Crenshaw, M. (1981) The Cause of Terrorism: Comparative Politics, Volume 13, Issue 4 (July 1981) 379-399. http://www.jstor.org.

48. Szczepanski, K. (n.d.) About Education: The Hukbalahap Rebellion in the Philippines. Retrieved: September 4, 2015. http://asianhistory.about.com/od/philippines/fl/The-Hukbalahap-Rebellion-in-the-Philippines.htm.

49. Seachon, A. L. (2004) Insurgencies in History: A Blueprint for Future Strategy. http://www.army.mil.ph/OG5_articles/Insegencies.htm.

50. Whitman, P. F. (n.d.) Corregidor Historic Society. The 503 PRCT Heritage Battalion Online: The Corregidor Massacre – 1968. Retrieved: November 28, 2012. http://www.corregidor.org/heritage_battalion/jabidah.html.

51. Global Security.org Website: Philippine Defense Spending. Retrieved: December 21, 2012. http://www.globalsecurity.org/military/world/philippines/budget.htm.

52. Yahoo News (December 20, 2015) Weeklong Assault Captures Extremist Camp, Claims 29 Lives: Philippines. Retrieved: December 21, 2015. https://sg.news.yahoo.com/week-: long-assault-captures-extremist-camp-claims-29-183315381.html.

53. Marcial, J. (February 8, 2008) Pilipino Express: A Year of Terror in a Philippine Jungle. Gracia Burnham, as interviewed by Janellyn Marcial of the Pilipino Express. http://www.pilipino-express.com/features/special-features/124-a-year-of-terror-in-a-philippine-jungle.html.

54. Unson, J. (September 11, 2013) *Philippine Star* Global Headline. Nur Misuari as Leader of the ARMM and MNLF. Retrieved: April 31, 2016.

    http://www.philstar.com/headlines/2013/09/11/1198131/nur-misuari-leader-armm-and-mnlf.

55. Pareno, R. (August 15, 2013) *Philippine Star*: "Nur Declares Independence of Bangsamoro Republic." Retrieved: September 10, 2013. http://www.philstar.com/nation/2013/08/15/1094161/nur-declares-independence-bangsamoro-republik.

56. Armstrong, P. and Swartz, T. (September 9, 2013) CNN: Muslim Rebels Hold 20 Hostages in Zamboanga City, Philippines. http://edition.cnn.com/2013/09/09/world/asia/philippines-muslim-rebels-unrest/.

57. Bautista, A. M. (October 5, 2011) News. Interaksyon: Two Moro Leaders Admit Kadaffi Funded MNLF, MILF Rebels 5. Retrieved: December 5, 2012. http://www.interaksyon.com/article/15860/2-moro-leaders-admit-gaddafi-funded-mnlf-milf-rebels.

58. Chalk, P. (November 26, 2013) Combating Terrorism Center: The Bangsamoro Islamic Freedom Fighters: The Newest Obstacles to Peace in the Southern Philippines? Retrieved: September 9,

2015. https://www.ctc.usma.edu/posts/the-bangsamoro-islamic-freedom-fighters-the-newest-obstacles-to-peace-in-the-southern-philippines.

59. Romero, P. (March 10, 2015) *Philippine Star*. Ph117 Billion to Be Allocated for BBL Implementation. Retrieved: May 2, 2016. http://www.philstar.com/headlines/2015/03/10/1431951/p117-b-be-allocated-bbl-implementation.

60. Atul, J. (n.d.) Preserve Articles. Retrieved: October 26, 2015. http://www.preservearticles.com/201105156651/love-of-money-root-of-evil.html.

61. God And Truth (March 9, 2009). Retrieved: May 3, 2016. http://www.godandtruth.com/gat_msg_ar223.htm.

62. Holy Bible (1 Timothy 6:10, NKJV).

63. Holy Bible (James:4:1, NKJV).

64. Arquillas, C. O. (February 14, 2011) *Mindanao News*:Lone Survivor of Jabidah Massacre Dies in Vehicular Accident. Retrieved: January 7, 2012.

65. Jaraula, C. G. (1997) Constitutions of the Philippines and Basic Documents: A Compilation with Commentaries. Mindanao Editorial & Printing Services, 93 Julio Pacana St., 9000 Cagayan de Oro City, Philippines.

66. Inquirer Research (October 8, 2012) *Philippine Daily Inquirer*. True or False: Was 1972 Enrile Ambush Faked? Retrieved: December 10, 2012. http://newsinfo.inquirer.net/284836/true-or-false-was-1972-enrile-ambush-fakedcitation.

67. Encyclopedia of World Biography.(n.d.) Benigno Aquino Biography. Retrieved: January 15, 2013. http://www.notablebiographies.com/An-Ba/Aquino-Benigno.html.

68. Casiple, M. (2012) Mon Casiple's Weblog: A Running Commentary on Philippine Politics. Anak ng Bayan. Retrieved: January 8, 2013. http://moncasiple.wordpress.com/.

69. Inquirer Global Nation Article (November 15, 2012 issue) The Home of Filipinos Worldwide: Filipino on FBI's Terror Wanted List. Retrieved: November 15, 2012. http://globalnation.inquirer.net/56340/filipino-on-fbis-terror-wanted-list.

70. The Manila Times.Net (January 7, 2013) Fate of Kidnap for Ransom Unknown. http://www.manilatimes.net/index.php/news/top-stories/38614-fate-of-many-kidnap-victims-unknown.

71. US Department of the Treasury (October 5, 2012) Press Center. Remarks of Undersecretary David Cohen at Chatham House on "Kidnapping for Ransom: The Growing Terrorist Financing Challenge." http://www.treasury.gov/press-center/press-releases/Pages/tg1726.aspx.

72. Kho, Madge (n.d.) Fighting the Abu Sayyaf: A Pretext for US Intervention in the Philippines. Retrieved: January 30, 30, 2013. http://www.philippineupdate.com/madge.htm.

73. Burnham, G. (2004) *In the Presence of My Enemies.* Tyndale House Publishing, 351 Executive Drive Carol Stream, IL 60188, United States (630) 784-5555.

74. Wood, J. (2011) PBS NewsHourWebsite: US Aid to Afghanistan Encouraging Dependency, Corruption. www.pbs.org/newshour/bb/military/jan-june11/Afghanistan1_06-08. html. Retrieved: November 30, 201264.

75. Covera, A. (2013) PHILSTAR.COM. The Filipino Global Community. *New York Times* Editorial: US Aid Helping Militants Because of AFP Corruption. http://www.philstar.com/headlines/224696/new-york-times-editorial-us-aid-helping-militants-because-afp-corruption.

76. GlobalSecurity.Org. (2012) Military: Philippine Defense Spending. Retrieved: January 9, 2013. http://www.globalsecurity.org/military/world/philippines/budget.htm.

77. Niksch, L. (n.d.) CRS Report for Congress Received through the CRS Web Order Code RL31265 Abu Sayyaf: Target of Philippine-US Antiterrorism Cooperation January 25, 2002.

78. GMA News Online, (February 12, 2011) Ex-Cabinet Execs: Corruption Killed Gen. Angelo Reyes. Retrieved: December 19, 2012. http://www.gmanetwork.com/news/story/212859/news/nation/ex-cabinet-execs-corruption-killed-gen-angelo-reyes#sthash.mjnsr1BU.dpuf.

79. Shah, A. (September 4, 2011) Global Issues: Corruption. Retrieved: September 9, 2015. http://www.globalissues.org/article/590/corruption.

80. ABS-CBNNews.Com (February 8, 2011). Retrieved: December 19, 2012. http://www.abs-cbnnews.com/anc/02/18/11/highlights-feb-18-senate-hearing-military-corruption.

81. *Sunstar* Website (February 19, 2011) Corruption Monitor: Aquino Backs Probe on Military Corruption. Retrieved: January 20, 2013. http://blogs.sunstar.com.ph/corruptionmonitor/2011/02/19/aquino-backs-probe-on-military-corruption/.

82. Ibrahim, A. (July 2009) Belfer Center for Science and International Affairs: US Aid to Pakistan: US Taxpayers Have Funded Pakistani Corruption. John F. Kennedy School of Government. Harvard University, July 2009. Retrieved: December 21, 2012. http://belfercenter.ksg.harvard.edu/publication/19490/us_aid_to_pakistanus_taxpayers_have_funded_pakistani_corruption.html.

83. S. Akbar Saidi (September 21, 2011, pp. 11–12) Carnegie Endowment. Policy Outlook: For International Peace Who Benefits from US Aid to Pakistan. Retrieved: December 21, 2012. http://www.carnegieendowment.org/files/pakistan_aid2011.pdf.

84. Hisona, H. (January 30, 2011) Philippine Almanac: Senator Trillanes Speaks on GMA's Possible Involvement in Military Corruption. http://www.philippinealmanac.com/news/senator-trillanes-speaks-on-gmas-possible-involvement-in-military-corruption-18110.html.

85. Trillanes IV, A. F. (October 2001) A Study of Corruption in the Philippine Navy. Retrieved: December 21, 2012. http://www.aibi.ph/politics/DOCS/TRILLANES%20-%20Corruption%20In%20The%20Philippine%20Navy.pdf.

86. *Sunstar* Corruption Monitor(March 22, 2011) Corruption Monitor: New witness in military corruption probe confirms older testimony. http://blogs.sunstar.com.ph/corruptionmonitor/2011/03/22/new-witness-in-military-corruption-probe-confirms-older-testimony/.

87. Ibid. February 7, 2011.

88. Felongco, G. (March 1, 2003) Gulf News.com Army gets 90 days to wipe out Abu Sayyaf. Retrieved: December 25, 2012. http://gulfnews.com/news/gulf/uae/general/army-gets-90-days-to-wipe-out-abu-sayyaf-1.348743.

89. GlobalSecurity.Org (n.d.) Military: Moro Islamic Liberation Front. Retrieved: January 30, 2013. http://www.globalsecurity.org/military/world/para/milf.htm.

90. Migrante Australia Website, (December 14, 2010) Commentary: Australian Military Assistance to the Philippines.

Retrieved: September 4, 2015. http://migrante.org.au/ australian-military-assistance-to-the-philippines/.

91. Mo g a to, M . (2 013) U . S . Tr i p l e s M i l i t a r y A i d to the Philippines in 2012 . Retrieved: August 10, 2015. http://w w w.reuters.com /a r t ic le / 2012/05 /03 / us-philippines-usa-idUSBRE8420IU2012050381.

92. DefenseNewsWebsite, (2015) The Philippines Seeks More Military A id to Counter China. Retrieved: Au g u st 20 , 2015 . http : // w w w. de f e nse ne w s . c om / s tory/defense /international /asia-pacif ic /2015 / 04 /21/ philippines-seeks-more-military-aid-to-counter-china/26148525/.

93. *Philippine Star*, (December 29, 2009) Opinion: Editorial - Mini Ampatuans. Retrieved: August 30, 2015. www.philstar.com/ opinion/536071/editorial-mini-ampatuans.

94. ABS-CBNNEWS.com, (December 07, 2009) Never Forget: Ampatuans Have Enough Guns For 2 Battalions. Retrieved: August 30, 2015. http://www.abs-cbnnews.com/nation/ regions/12/07/09/ampatuans-have-enough-guns-2-batallions.

95. Lingao, E. (February 3, 2010) The Maguindanao Chronicles: The Philippine Center for Investigative Journalism; Reports on Politics, Murder, and the Quest for Justice. Why Poor Maguindanao Is Awash with Weapons of War. Ampatuans Used Public Office to Amass Mostly Illegal Guns. Retrieved: September 1, 2015. http://pcij.org/stories/ ampatuans-used-public-office-to-amass-mostly-illegal-guns/.

96. GlobalSecurity.Org, (n.d.). Military: Philippine Defense Spending. Retrieved: September 8, 2015. http://www.globalsecurity.org/ military/world/philippines/budget.htm.

97. GAO. US Government Accountability Office. Southeast Asia. Better Human Rights Reviews and Strategic Planning Needed for U.S. Assistance to Foreign Security Forces. http://www.gao.gov/ products/GAO-05-79390.

98. Master, T. M. (2009) The Link between Moral Anger and Social Activism: An Exploratory Study. New Brunswick, New Jersey.

99. A S I A N E W S . I t (De c e m be r 26 , 2 012) Mu s l i m Pol i t i c i a n f rom M i nd a na o : C at hol i c E duc at i on Helped Me in the Commitment to Peace. Retrieved: December 26, 2012. http://www.asianews.it/news-en/

Muslim-Politician-from-Mindanao:-Catholic-education-helped-me-in-the-commitment-to-peace-16805.html.

100. Lindsay, H. (2002, p.119) The Everlasting Hatred: The Roots of Jihad. Oracle House Publishing, Murrieta, 92562.

101. Cal, B. (October 9, 2012) BALITA October 10, 1977 Patikul Massacre Recalled (featured) balita.ph/2012/10/09/oct-10-1977-patikul-massacre-recalled-featured/.

102. Zakaria, F. (September 11, 2012) CNN WORLD: Al-Qaeda Diminished, But Not Gone. http://globalpublicsquare.blogs.cnn.com/2012/09/11/al-qaeda-diminished-but-not-gone/Retrieved: December 26, 201294.

103. Wright, L. (2007, pp. 226–227) The Looming Tower. Al Qaeda and the Road to 9/11. First Vintage Books Edition September 2007. www.vintagebooks.com.

104. Inquirer Global Nations Website Article. Retrieved: January 5, 2013. www.globalnation.inquirer.net/4979/philippines-get- 12m-in gear- from-us-.for- war-in-terror-fight.

==

To God Be the Glory